I'll Tell You
A Story,
I'll Sing You
A Song

I'll Tell You A Story, I'll Sing You A Song

— CHRISTINE ALLISON —

A Parents' Guide to the Fairy Tales,
Fables, Songs, and Rhymes of Childhood

Delacorte Press/New York

Published by
Delacorte Press
The Bantam Doubleday Dell Publishing Group, Inc.
1 Dag Hammarskjold Plaza
New York, New York 10017

Designed by Sheree Goodman

Manufactured in the United States of America

First printing

Library of Congress Cataloging in Publication Data
Allison, Christine.
I'll tell you a story, I'll sing you a song.
Summary: A collection of fairy tales, nursery rhymes, fables, and songs of childhood, with discussions of how a parent can effectively introduce them to children.
1. Children's literature.   [1. Literature—Collections]
I. Title
PZ5.A48I1   1987   87–9074
ISBN 0-385-29569-3

Grateful acknowledgment is made for permission to reprint from the following:

"It's Raining, It's Pouring" and "Bluebird, Bluebird"
From *Sally Go Round the Sun* by Edith Fowke. Used by permission of the Canadian publishers McClelland and Stewart Limited, Toronto.

"Blue-Tail Fly"
Arranged by Burl Ives © copyright 1944, 1945 by MCA Music Publishing, a division of MCA Inc., New York, New York. Copyright renewed. Used by permission. All rights reserved.

"All the Pretty Little Horses"
Collected, adapted and arranged by John A. Lomax and Alan Lomax. TRO © copyright 1934 and renewed 1962 Ludlow Music, Inc., New York, New York. Used by permission.

"Au Clair de la Lune"
From *The Baby's Songbook* by Elizabeth Poston (Thomas Y. Crowell) copyright © 1971 by Elizabeth Poston. Reprinted by permission of Harper & Row Publishers, Inc.

"Thank You for the World So Sweet"
By Mrs. E. Rutter Leatham, which appears in *Songs of Praise,* Enlarged Edition, copyright 1926, ninth impression 1944. Permission granted by Mrs. Lorna Hill on behalf of the copyright owner.

"Roll Over"
Reprinted by permission of Sterling Publishing Co., Inc., Two Park Avenue, New York, New York 10016, from *The Silly Songbook* by Esther L. Nelson, copyright 1981 by Esther L. Nelson.

"Pawpaw Patch"
Reprinted by permission of Sterling Publishing Co., Inc., Two Park Avenue, New York, New York 10016, from *The Best Singing Games for Children of All Ages* by Edgar S. Bley, copyright 1957 by Sterling Publishing Co., Inc.

To my mother and my father,
and to Knute, wherever you are

ACKNOWLEDGMENTS

Thanks, in gigantic measure, to Molly Wade McGrath, who spent months helping to retell the fables and fairy tales and assisted in the researching and writing. Beth Puffer combed the libraries and talked to parents and teachers to help us determine the most memorable of everything: songs, stories, and rhymes. Rosalie Holzman, early childhood educator, shed enormous light. So did the extraordinary storyteller Diane Wolkstein, who granted us a most illuminating interview. Peter Dunlop and Jean Thomas, who were born storytellers, gave great guidance. Dr. Mary Jett-Simpson's book, **Parenting and Beginning Reading** *(Humanics Limited, Atlanta, Georgia, 1984), was an enormous help and I recommend it. Particular thanks also to Holly Rivlin of Eeyore's Books for Children in New York City; Learning Ladders Catalogue in Scarsdale, New York; and Elizabeth Long, Senior Children's Librarian at the General Library of the Performing Arts at Lincoln Center, New York Public Library.*

I am deeply indebted to Patty Brown for her keen editorial judgment and occasional, when desperately needed, wisecracks. Also to John Boswell, for being my mentor. Both Patty and John and family and friends racked their brains for many of the verses and lyrics in this book, and their help was invaluable. Sue Lorimer kept me on course. Gary Luke kept the book on course. Emily Reichert was the kind of editor an author dreams about: enthusiastic, caring, and smart. St. Teresa, thank you. And finally, mostly, thank you to Wick, Gillea, and Maisie. For listening.

Contents

INTRODUCTION

"A child will love
anyone who will
help him to perfect
his spirit."
—Maria Montessori,
A Child in the Family

One of the happier surprises we encounter as new parents is that for the first time we have an audience.

Someone who, without judgment, without even question, listens to the trials of our day.

Someone who actually likes our jokes.

Someone who, amazingly, responds with rapture to our songs and our stories.

This book is about *you* and your little audience. It is about one of the most natural aspects of parenting, the telling of stories and the singing of songs. Because no matter how shy or tone-deaf you seem to be, no matter what you've read or what your mother told you, you are now officially a singer and a storyteller.

And if you, like me, became a new parent in the past decade, you are a singer and a storyteller with a very basic problem.

The problem is, we can't remember the words.

I came to realize this when my first daughter was just a few months old.

I had entered her nursery one evening at twilight; it was a pink-and-blue heaven. She was awake and, to my mind, perfect. After a few coos and a handful of silly faces, I decided a song was in order. I chose "Brahms' Lullaby." This is what came out:

Lullaby, and good night
Da Da Dee Da Da Dee Dee
Da Da Da Daa
Da Da Daa
Da Da Da Da Da Dee Dee

It was not a memorable performance. It was, however, just the beginning of my troubles, for the more I ventured into the world of song, the more I became aware of my own peculiar amnesia. A diabolical situation had developed whereby I could recall the first lines of all of my favorite songs and the second lines of none of them.

Storytelling proved an even more dismal foray. I left Jack stranded at the top of the beanstalk. My Snow White could not name the Seven Dwarfs. I knew all of the psychological ramifications of Red Riding Hood's unfortunate encounter with the wolf, but I could not for the life of me figure how she eluded him. Nursery rhymes, which are so important for toddlers, just didn't get said.

As a singer and a storyteller, I was bombing.

And I soon discovered that mine was not an isolated experience. Most new parents have forgotten the words, plots, and characters to the great treasures of Western literature and song and for a simple reason: We start our families later in life. For centuries parents were virtually kids themselves and, only a few years before, had stopped listening to tales and chanting along with rhymes. Nowadays we put two, sometimes three, decades between our childhood and our parenthood, and we cram a lot in between. Small wonder that our Jacks get waylaid on beanstalks and that other, fairly intolerable inconveniences beset our heroes and heroines, who are mainly victims of our forgetfulness.

This is a sorry state of affairs but not for reasons of sentiment. The oral tradition is not just a quaint throwback to Chaucer or the Bible or Aesop, nor is it the mere lack of paper and pencil. It is, quite simply, the most powerful means of human communication. And for that reason it will survive our forgetfulness and videocassettes and pop-up books, because nothing can enchant a child—or an adult—like a story well told or a song that is sung at the right moment.

The spoken word has its own power, and it carries a mysteriousness that cannot be duplicated by the word that is read aloud. It arises from nowhere, from the invisible—from the heart, the memory, and the imagination. If we look back to our own childhood memories and hear a parent or a teacher or our oldest, dearest aunt telling us a tale, we can recall the quality of the voice, the experience of following the teller into an untraveled land. It is an extraordinary adventure.

The voice that does not read obediently from the page is powerful in another way, for it carries a sense of authority. It is believable. A child hears an account of "Rapunzel," and it is as if the teller might have been there, to know so well how she looked, how she felt, and what was said. Anything is possible in the listener's mind because anything is possible in the teller's mind, and the greatest, most amazing possibility of all is that it might be utterly true.

This is not to detract from the value of *reading aloud.* In fact, more and more we are documenting the benefits of reading aloud to children and the imperative to do so with regularity from as early as the age of six months. We also know that as infants turn into toddlers, they find the illustrations in children's books become an unduplicable means of identifying with the emerging world around them. By the same token, great literature is not to be told but read aloud. Even the finest storyteller would be presumptuous to tackle *Jane Eyre.*

But there is a bank of stories and verses that were created to be "told." These fairy tales and fables and rhymes endured *because* of storytellers (often parents), and it is this particular brand of literature that I have gathered in this book. And when we recall that the value of reading aloud is that it stimulates bonding and awakens a love for reading, we see that storytelling takes these advantages one step further.

As storytellers, we are suddenly holding the essence of a story, in all of its glory, inside us. In giving it to our child, with free hands and a free voice and free eyes, we intensify bonding and the imaginative qualities of our presentation. The arts that were used with success on virtually every generation before us can be ours. Storytelling is but one of them. Singing is another, for just as the spoken word stirs the child's imagination with extraordinary force, the word that is sung affects his emotions, and astoundingly so. To hear one's mother sing "Amazing Grace" is a most soothing experience for a child of any age, if not one of the great privileges in life. Likewise, "Yankee Doodle" can create a brightness, an internal march of the spirit, so that the child who is bored on a rainy afternoon can harken to a melody when nothing else might have moved him. The parent who surprises his child with the right song at the right moment gives rise to the richest memories of childhood.

I'll Tell You a Story, I'll Sing You a Song is a primer for new parents on how to use and remember the stories and verses and songs of childhood. It is a book that was first born of my forgetfulness but that finally came into being when I realized that the only surefire tool in parenting is magic. As I gathered the fairy tales and songs and fables and rhymes, I learned how to use these gems to kindle my daughter's imagination, to soothe her, and to develop her ability to be alert to the world.

Meanwhile psychologists and child-development researchers have underlined the value of conserving storytelling and singing techniques for children as young as three months. In the past nine years studies have shown that both art forms are crucial to:

- the development of your child's imagination
- your child's ability to conceptualize
- the parent-child bonding process
- the discipline of listening, paying attention, focusing
- the mastery of language skills.

To that end, I have not only gathered fairy tales, nursery rhymes, fables, songs, motion songs, lullabies and prayers, but also have sought to share some counsel on how best to use the oral tradition in parenting.

I'll Tell You a Story, I'll Sing You a Song does not presume to be an end-all book on storytelling but rather a modest beginning. It does not aim to make a maestro out of your child but rather to help you share the gift of melody.

It is for the person who wants to take a pause from the modern age—the noise and gimmicks and parental dos and don'ts—and just have fun. It is for the parent who has felt an urge to sing to his child, just as surely as he has wanted to embrace him. It is for the monkey in us, the good witch in us, the gremlin in us, and—of course—the ham.

And it is for those of us who believe that a life without fairies is not worth living.

HOW TO USE THIS BOOK

You already know everything in this book.

You have already been to Cinderella's ball; you have already seen them try to put Humpty back together again; you've skipped to your Lou. There are no surprises in this book. I have not chosen one fairy tale in which you could not at least visualize the characters. I have not included any song that you could not at least hum. Nor will you encounter any nursery rhyme that seems odd. This is the stuff we grew up with, and it is the stuff we want to share with our children, just as surely as we want them to know baseball and Bach.

As it happens, I am a big believer in selectivity; I am a snob. I contend that "you are what you sing" or "tell," as it were. Be choosy. Tell only those stories you love or those fables that hit home. Don't sing "Frère Jacques" if it doesn't strike you as delightful, or "Little Bo Peep" if you are troubled by her ridiculous name. If you don't have a funny bone in your body, avoid nonsense rhymes; they will make you very uncomfortable. If you can't keep a straight face, you will botch "Au Clair de la Lune," so leave that to others. Build your own repertoire and use this book as a starting point. Your child will not remember your omissions but who you were and what life is because of what you chose to share.

They say timing is everything, and in obeisance to that theory I have put tiny symbols throughout the book: a moon, a sun, a duck, a spoon, and a wheel. These elements represent the things you do with your child or help your child to do: sleeping, waking, bathing, feeding, and traveling. For the most part these activities compose the bulk of daily life until our children start school. If you choose, you can use with great effect the stories and rhymes and songs that follow, timed to the various activities. (My first daughter's first words were, "Row, row, row" because I used to sing "Row, Row, Row Your Boat" before her bath. True, I would have preferred a heartfelt "Mama," but what are you going to do?)

You will see that each chapter has short essays scattered throughout, with guidance on how to use the surrounding material as well as some basic background for your edification. You don't have to read them all at once, but they will give you suggestions on how to stimulate your child's intelligence and imagination and still have fun.

A serious word about fun.

For all of the counsel we get (and need) on subjects such as diapers and temper tantrums and sibling rivalry, an omission in our schooling has affected us as parents, and that is the value of pure fun. As you master the storytelling basics you will find yourself warmed by the sound of your inner voice, the new command you have of words and ideas, and the grandness of theater itself. The dullness of any routine will be washed away when you break out with a rousing "Oh, Susanna." Your child's sleepy head on a crisp, white pillow will be even more beautiful when you sing "All Through the Night."

So this is art, and this is beauty, and this is fun.

Now, when you tell a story or sing a song, make it an event; close the doors on the rest of the world. Your child will be keenly aware that you are all his or hers, and together you will enter a fantasy world, a place of your own making. This is truly a romantic adventure, and, most important, it is an adventure that will *never* escape the memory of your child.

Indeed I remember, a few years ago, my father exclaiming in our busy kitchen, "If only I had been a poet." My father is a finance executive for a major corporation, and I suppose he was feeling the weight of numbers that afternoon. It was a funny statement, because all of his children always suspected that he had, at the very least, the soul of a poet. This is because when we were little, he used to tell us about his buddy Knute. He and Knute were adventurers and (presumably before my father met my mother, it was never clear) they had traveled to Africa, the South Seas, the moon, back in time, and to other suspiciously remote places like that. The twosome were always caught in bizarre entanglements, fighting for their survival. Over and again, the astonished enemy would have to yield to their ingenuity or to their virtue. However homespun, this was poetry. And the times my father took to share the world of his own making—his travels with Knute—are the most unforgettable of my childhood.

That said, let us begin. If I have done my job well, this book will serve as your cue card: the prompter who sits backstage in the shadows, reminding you of the treasures you want to share with your children. Whether you consult these pages once a day or once a week or once a month, I beg you not to leave them on the shelf too long.

But move along now. Your audience is waiting.

CHAPTER ONE

Fairy Tales

"I knew the magic beanstalk before I tasted beans;
I was sure of the Man in the Moon
before I was certain of the moon . . ."
—G. K. Chesterton, *Orthodoxy*

INTRODUCTION

Ｗe can presume that fairy tales are as old as fairies themselves. Fairies were more or less a creation of the Celts, but they were not really creatures to be reckoned with until the thirteenth century, when the Irish and the Welsh storytelling schools dominated the movement of the oral tradition and filled children's heads with visions of them. Still, the supernatural, which is what fairy tales are mostly about, has been discussed in story form throughout the ages. Fairy tales have been with us for a good while, and as long as we have childhood we will have the widened eyes of children transfixed by pixies.

The best-known fairy tales were created by Charles Perrault and Hans Christian Andersen and were collected by the Brothers Grimm. Perrault and Andersen seized on the oral tradition of their respective times and places and claimed the stories as their own by the simple eloquence of their own style and language. The Brothers Grimm were not writers but lawyers who spent their professional lives obsessed with collecting tales from the German countryside, laboring over language and detail, recording the tales in current circulation as honestly and accurately as they could. All fairy tales, as we know them, are distillations, and literally hundreds of versions of each basic story exist (e.g., there are four hundred versions of "Cinderella"). For the purposes of this book, we have presented the most commonly known plot lines and, in some cases, have given you variations to consider; but for the most part these are the "Americanized" versions, those common to our collective memory.

Fairy tales differ from folktales in that they usually call upon some form of magic or supernatural force to redeem or crush the main characters. A few of the entries in this section might better be described as folktales ("Stone Soup," "The Three Bears," etc.), but the distinction is not terribly important. In a fairy tale we find a handful of archetypal characters who are intermittently saved and battered by the forces of good and evil. These characters are generally everyday people (even kings seem ordinary in fairy tales) who are thrust into extraordinary circumstances, the result, most often, of having shown up for life that day. Our heroes and villains have so little dimension that they are rarely given full names, and what names they do have are throwaway: Jack, the Fisherman, Tom, and so on. But just for having gone to market or out to fish or, in some instances, just for having been born, these

3

simple folks encounter wild creatures and forces and trials, the likes of which are almost unfathomable. Unless you are a child.

Children, not surprisingly, can comprehend fairy tales with amazing perceptiveness. The story of an ordinary wee person overcome by gigantic unexplainable forces hits home. They take from these stories a very grand lesson: that life is not a fairy tale but harder and better. They learn that there are happy endings but that happiness isn't what life is all about. They learn that life is wrought by the forces of good and evil and that good is the clear choice; indeed, the only choice if one seeks a meaningful survival.

These are hard, but invigorating, truths for children, because they now know what to expect. Fairy tales give children the rules of the game. They are thus ready for mishap or miracle, and they are armed with the most profoundly pat answer in life: that it is always better to side with good. It almost makes parenting redundant.

Bruno Bettelheim, the brilliant child psychologist, discusses the importance of fairy tales in *The Uses of Enchantment,* a book which I recommend heartily. He suggests that children can come to terms with their anxieties and fears by projecting their causes onto the evil characters in fairy tales and, in doing so, take the crucial first step in isolating these anxieties and conquering them. Children use the "bad guys" in these stories as a point of focus to make their anxieties more manageable. They are free to jeer at the mean stepsisters in "Cinderella" when they might not be able to express resentment toward their own siblings without guilt and confusion. They can live through these stories to experience the rumble of their subconscious without fear of consequence. Fairy tales, he suggests, can cure.

It would be an awful thing if these marvelous tales were relegated to the status of merely being "good for you," like spinach or sturdy shoes, and, of course, this is not my point. But knowing that they are "healthy" does lend a happy urgency to the task of telling them. So let us tell them.

The secret to telling a fairy tale (or any tale) is to know that you are presenting a mystery, as in something mysterious. In *A Passage to India* the amazing Mrs. Moore makes this distinction: "I like mysteries, but I rather dislike muddles." These words speak not only to life but to the way we tell fairy tales. The mystery must be the message, and the message must never be muddled.

On page 43, you will find an exercise most useful in remembering these tales, and you will learn that the key to avoiding all sorts of muddles is to prepare yourself and your story with care.

You will find that the plot line is the most important element of any fairy tale; the characters, as I mentioned before, are all purposefully flat—it is their travails that make the story. To that end, each fairy tale in this book emphasizes the plot line and the key phrases.

The language in the stories that follow is reduced for two reasons. The first is that this book is about remembering, as much as it is about telling and singing. The plot lines are presented for you to remember and to absorb and embellish upon. Secondly, this is a book for beginning storytellers. As a beginner, it is the plot line that serves as the springboard for your ultimate presentation. Start with the bare bones of the story, then add your own flesh and trimmings. Once you have mastered the techniques, you can pursue original Grimms' tales and the like.

Do not be surprised if your child does in fact ask you to repeat a story over and over (and over) again; this is to be expected. And when you find yourself in this wonderful situation, you must try to keep the story intact with each telling; do not vary the words a bit. This is difficult, I know, but the story, to your child, has become a living, tangible thing, and to alter it in any way would disappoint and even confuse. Preserve your story as you would a work of art. It *is* one.

If you feel tempted to hold this book before you as you tell your story, *resist.* The idea is to maintain as much eye contact and visual concentration as is possible. Bettelheim contends that having a book between you and your audience is an encumbrance. I applaud his orthodoxy. I realize that when starting out, you will be a bit clumsy and eager for the security of a page, but I do encourage you to work to the point of telling your story solo. Distinguish the read-aloud event from the storytelling event; they are two completely different enterprises. The storytelling event is geared to stoking your child's imagination. There should be no illustrations to inhibit his visions, nor should pages stand in the way of the communion of teller and audience.

Try it. Try telling these fairy tales as soon as you can; as early in your child's life as possible. Take advantage of the fact that Nature, in her wisdom, has provided you with at least two years of rehearsal before your child has any sense of your garbled words or untame descriptions or inevitable tangents.

Do not be afraid to create magic. Do not be discouraged if something so worthwhile does not come with the sweep of the wand.

And now, without further ado, the tales you knew once upon a time.

THE THREE BEARS

nce upon a time there were three bears who lived together in their own small house in the woods.

One of them was a little wee bear, and one was a middle-sized bear. The other was a great big bear. They each had a bowl for their porridge—a little wee bowl for the little wee bear; a middle-sized bowl for the middle-sized bear, and a great big bowl for the great big bear. They each had a chair to sit on, just the right size for each of them. And they each had a bed that was just right too.

One morning, after they had made porridge for their breakfast, the three bears decided to take a walk while the porridge cooled. While they were gone, a little girl called Goldilocks came to their house. She looked through the window, and when she saw there was nobody inside, she went right in. The porridge on the table looked very good. First she tasted the porridge in the great big bear's bowl, but it was too hot. The porridge in the middle-sized bear's bowl was too cold. Then she tasted the porridge in the little wee bear's bowl, and it was just right. It tasted so good that Goldilocks ate it all up.

Then Goldilocks wandered into the parlor. There she found three different chairs. First she tried the big bear's chair, but it was too hard. Then she sat down in the middle bear's chair, but it was too soft. Finally she sat in the little bear's chair, and it was just right. But she was too heavy for it, and she fell right through the seat.

Up Goldilocks went to the bedroom where the three bears slept. There she found three beds. She tried each in turn. The big bear's bed was too high. The middle bear's bed was too low. And, once again, the little wee bear's bed was just right. Goldilocks felt so comfortable that she pulled up the covers, set her head on the pillow, and fell fast asleep.

Soon the three bears returned from their walk, thinking their porridge must have cooled. When the big bear looked in his porridge bowl and saw the spoon standing in it, he said, "Somebody has been tasting my porridge." The middle-sized bear looked in her porridge bowl and saw the spoon standing in it. "Somebody has been tasting *my* porridge," she said. Then the little wee bear looked at his porridge bowl and said, "Somebody has been tasting my porridge and has eaten it all up!"

In the parlor, the big bear noticed that the cushion in his favorite chair was disturbed and shouted, "Somebody has been sitting in my chair." The middle-sized bear saw that her chair had been disturbed too. The little wee bear took one look at his chair and declared, "Somebody has been sitting in my chair and has broken the seat!"

Upstairs, the big bear and middle-sized bear noticed that somebody had been lying in each of their beds. The little wee bear went straight to his bed and said, "Somebody has been lying in my bed, and here she is!"

Goldilocks awoke to see the three bears all staring at her. She was so frightened that she tumbled out of bed and jumped from the nearest window. She landed on the ground with a thump, and she ran away as fast as she could, and she never returned to the house of the three bears again.

STONE SOUP

Long, long ago in a foreign land, some soldiers were returning home from war. They had traveled far and were very tired and hungry. They kept thinking how much they would enjoy a nice bowl of soup, but they had nothing to make soup with—that is, they joked, unless soup could be made from the stones they were finding in the road along the way.

Eventually they saw a village up ahead. They mused about how happy they would be if the villagers would offer them a loaf of bread or a comfortable bed to sleep in, but they knew the villagers would be wary of them as soldiers and would not want to share what they had with strangers.

They were right about that. No sooner did the villagers catch sight of the soldiers in the distance than they hid all their food away and barred their windows. When the soldiers went knocking on doors in the hopes of finding some food and a place to sleep, they were told there was no food and there was no place to sleep.

Things looked very grim for the soldiers, until one of them had a bright idea. He said to the villagers, "I know you have no food to spare, but perhaps you will lend us a big cooking pot so we can make stone soup."

The villagers were very curious to know how stone soup was made. They watched with interest as the soldiers built a fire under the pot and searched about for what they called "good soup stones." They gathered around as the water boiled over the stones. Finally one of the soldiers had a good sniff. "Something's missing," he declared. One of the other soldiers suggested that some salt and pepper might help. Very politely he said to the villagers, "We understand that you have no food to spare, but if you could give us just a bit of salt and pepper, that would help our soup so much." The mayor's wife was glad to oblige. She went off like a shot and was back again soon with salt and pepper. The soldiers expressed their gratitude effusively, saying how much the salt and pepper had improved the soup.

And so it went. The soldiers would sniff the soup and politely observe how much better it would taste if it just had a few onions, a few stalks of celery, a handful of carrots, a potato or two, some barley to thicken it, some milk to enrich it. Each time they expressed a need for a certain ingredient, they would shake their heads ruefully and agree that they were hoping for too much. There was no use wishing for what you could not have. And each time one of the villagers would slip away quietly and come back with whatever ingredient was called for.

The soup began to smell more and more tantalizing. One of the soldiers observed that if there were a few chunks of meat in it, it would smell just like the soup they'd made for the king a few weeks ago. The villagers were astonished that these soldiers had dined with the king. They hurried to their houses and came back with big hunks of meat, which they added eagerly to the soup. When the soup had cooked long enough, the soldiers tasted it and pronounced it delicious. The townspeople were so excited about this extraordinary stone soup that they brought all kinds of food out of hiding to go with it. There seemed to be enough food and drink for a feast. So the villagers and the soldiers sat down at long tables in the middle of the village to enjoy it. After the meal there was great frolicking and dancing in the street. The soldiers were invited to sleep in comfortable beds in the villagers' homes.

The next morning, everyone arose early to see the soldiers on their way. The soldiers thanked the mayor and the villagers for their generosity, and the mayor thanked the soldiers for teaching them how to make such extraordinary soup.

After the soldiers were gone, the villagers remarked among themselves that it was all pretty amazing. Who would ever imagine that stone soup could taste so good?

The Brothers Grimm

Jakob and Wilhelm Grimm were born just a year apart, in 1785 and 1786, at Hanau in Hesse-Cassel, Germany, during a period of great political turbulence. They were two of six children whose father, a lawyer, died when they were all quite young.

When they were older, Jakob and Wilhelm chose to study law as their father had done, hoping that their studies would lead to opportunities to make a better world for Europeans. While attending the University of Marburg they met the famous law professor and scholar, Friedrich Karl von Savigny, who introduced them to the legends of the Middle Ages and the German Minnesingers—the poet singers of the twelfth, thirteenth, and fourteenth centuries. Though the boys continued their law studies and became librarians, they decided that in addition to their professional activities, their life's work lay in seeking out, deciphering, and editing manuscripts from the Middle Ages.

The manuscripts that interested them most were those of fairy tales. They supplemented these with folktales that had been told for centuries. Frau Katherina Viehmann was a well-known teller of these tales when the Brothers Grimm discovered her in 1811. Nineteen of the tales in the Grimms' collection were attributed to Frau Viehmann, better known as "the story-wife of Niederzwehren," the small town near Cassel where she lived with her husband, a tailor. "This woman," Wilhelm Grimm wrote in the preface to the first edition of the second volume of Grimms' tales (1815) ". . . retains fast in mind these old sagas—which talent, as she says, is not granted to everyone. . . ."

The Brothers Grimm were very different: Wilhelm was gay and gentle; Jakob was studious, disciplined, and lived with his head in his manuscripts most of the time. But the two were rarely separated throughout their lives. They slept in the same bed when they were children and worked at the same table. As students, they shared a room with two beds and two tables. Even after Wilhelm's marriage in 1825, there was always a room in the house for Jakob.

Gathering the tales was a labor of love for the brothers. In a time of tremendous political upheaval, Jakob and Wilhelm devoted themselves to resurrecting the best of the past to create a brighter future. In his writing Wilhelm mentioned "foreign persons, foreign manners, and a foreign, loudly spoken language" in their thorough-fares, "and poor people staggering along the streets, being led away to death." Jakob worked at a small clerkship in the War Office. Two of their other brothers were in the field with the hussars. Wilhelm suffered from a severe heart disorder, but whenever possible, the two brothers worked together at the task of keeping the folklore of Europe alive.

Volume one of the tales the Grimms had gathered, entitled *Kinder und Hausmarchen (Nursery and Household Tales)* was published in the winter of Napoleon's retreat from Moscow (1812). In Vienna the book was banned as a work of superstition. Elsewhere, in spite of all the political tension in the air, it was warmly received. Critics called the book the masterpiece of the Romantic movement in Germany. A second volume was published in 1815 and a third in 1822. Revisions and annotated editions followed at regular intervals until the brothers died, first Wilhelm, in 1859, and just a few years later, Jakob, in 1863.

THE THREE BILLY GOATS GRUFF

nce there were three billy goats who wanted to go to a beautiful meadow where the grass was green and there was plenty for them to eat.

To get to the meadow they had to cross over a small bridge. Under the bridge lived a mean old troll who didn't want anyone crossing his bridge. The three billy goats put their minds to thinking how they might outwit him. Finally they decided to send the littlest billy goat off first.

Clip-clippety, clip-clippety, went the baby goat's hooves across the bridge.

"Who is crossing over my bridge?" shouted the troll.

"It's just me," the little billy goat replied.

"Oh, no, you don't. No one is allowed to cross my bridge without permission and you did, so I'm going to eat you up."

The little billy goat pointed out to the troll that his brother would be coming along soon and he was bigger and would taste better. The troll agreed to let the youngest billy goat go on.

The second billy goat came by and had much the same discussion with the troll, eventually persuading him to wait for the third billy goat, who was big and fat and would taste absolutely delicious. The troll let the middle billy goat go, too, and waited impatiently for his brother.

As soon as he heard the sound of the big billy goat's hooves on the bridge, the troll asked who was crossing over his bridge and bounded up to meet the third billy goat. Without bothering to reply to the troll's question, the big billy goat booted the troll neatly on the rear end with his horns and sent him somersaulting into the river below. The troll was never heard from again, and the three Billy Goats Gruff had a lovely summer frolicking in the grassy meadow.

How to Light a Story

One of the greatest challenges faced by the oral tradition was not the printing press but the invention of the light bulb. In Europe especially, the light bulb dealt a nasty blow to the storyteller, who in villages everywhere used to arrive "with the coming of night" to cast his spells. When the light bulb arrived, the storyteller seemed out of place; people were too busy reading and sewing and mending to need his entertainment.

The important lesson for modern-day storytellers is to remember the power of twilight. Never tell a story in a brightly lit room; you will illuminate too many distractions. Conversely, a completely blackened room removes all eye contact from your presentation and thus is unacceptable. You will do best to light a room on the darker side of gray.

One of the most enchanting customs I know of is the "wishing candle," a little ceremony used quite often by librarians when they are telling a story. To introduce a wishing candle, simply light the candle at the beginning of your tale and quietly blow it out at the tale's end. You will add immeasurable drama and theater to your presentation, and your child will love it.

THE FROG PRINCE

ong ago there was a beautiful princess who often amused herself by throwing her golden ball in the air as she sat by a cool well in the forest. One day the ball came down near the edge of the well and rolled in. The well was so deep that she despaired of ever seeing it again. She began to weep, and as she did so, she heard a voice say, "What is it, lovely princess? Why are you so sad?"

She looked up and saw that the voice came from a fat old frog who had stuck his head up out of the water. She told the frog why she was weeping. He asked what she would give him if he would fetch the ball for her, and she replied, "Whatever you like, dear frog." He said he wasn't interested in her finery, her jewels, or even her golden crown. He wanted the right to be her companion and playfellow. Thinking the frog could never do anything but sit in the water and croak, she agreed to his proposal. In no time at all he swam to the bottom of the well, retrieved the princess's golden ball, and returned to the surface with it in his mouth. Delighted, the princess bounded away, forgetting all about the frog.

The following evening while the king and his family were having dinner, there was a knock on the door and a voice called out, "Princess, let me in!" It was the frog wanting to claim his share of the bargain. The princess was somewhat taken aback, but when she explained what the frog wanted to her father, the king said she must keep her word. The princess was obliged to allow the frog to sit next to her and even eat from her golden plate. After he'd feasted heartily the frog announced that he was weary and would like to go to sleep—in the princess's bed!

The king insisted that the princess keep her promise, but she could not bring herself to allow the cold, clammy frog to share her silken bed with her. She put him in a corner of her bedroom, but he crept to her, begging to be taken into the bed. In a moment of pity she picked him up and kissed him, saying, "You poor, poor frog. What will I do with you?"

With that the frog became a handsome prince with beautiful eyes. He told her how a wicked witch had placed a spell on him from which she had released him. Eventually the king gave permission for his daughter and the prince to be married. They were carried off in a splendid carriage with eight white horses to the prince's palace, where they lived happily ever after.

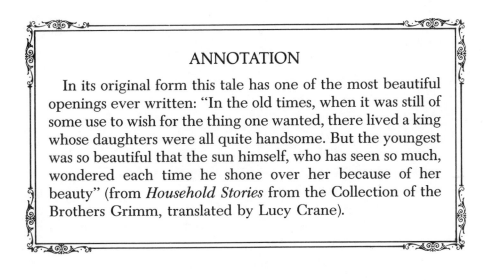

ANNOTATION

In its original form this tale has one of the most beautiful openings ever written: "In the old times, when it was still of some use to wish for the thing one wanted, there lived a king whose daughters were all quite handsome. But the youngest was so beautiful that the sun himself, who has seen so much, wondered each time he shone over her because of her beauty" (from *Household Stories* from the Collection of the Brothers Grimm, translated by Lucy Crane).

THE LITTLE RED HEN

An industrious little red hen worked hard taking care of her family. One day, when she was out walking with her friends the goose, the cat, and the pig, she found a few grains of wheat lying in the grass.

"Who will plant this wheat?" she asked her friends.

"Not I," said the goose.

"Not I," said the cat.

"Not I," said the pig.

"Very well," said the little red hen. "Then I will." And she did.

In a short time the wheat sprouted and grew to be tall and yellow.

"Who will help me harvest the wheat?" said the little red hen when the wheat was ripe for cutting. Once again, the goose, the cat, and the pig all said, "Not I." And the little red hen did it herself.

When it was time to thresh the wheat, the little red hen again asked who would help, and she received the same response. When the wheat was all threshed, the little red hen poured it into large sacks and said, "Who'll take this wheat to the mill to be ground into flour?

"Not I," said the goose.

"Not I," said the cat and the pig in turn.

The little red hen said she'd do it herself. And she did.

"Who will make this flour into bread?" the little red hen asked the next day. Her friends responded in the usual way.

When the bread was baked, the little red hen took it out of the oven, golden and sweet-smelling. "Who will eat this lovely bread?" she called out to her friends.

"I will!" said the goose.

"I will!" said the cat.

"I will!" said the pig.

"That's what you think," said the little red hen. "I planted this wheat and watched it grow. I cut it and threshed it and took it to the mill in heavy sacks to be ground into flour. Finally I made this beautiful loaf of bread, and I am going to eat it all myself." And so she did.

ANNOTATION

In another version of the story a cock and a mouse live together with the little red hen in a pretty house. Early in the story it appears that the little red hen does most of the work around the house. The other two reply, "I won't," to her suggestions that they lend a hand.

The little red hen's requests for help are met almost instantly when the issue becomes that of escaping from the fox, who attempts to kidnap them in a large sack. Following the little red hen's instructions, the animals escape from the sack, fill it with rocks instead, and scurry home to safety. Instead of three juicy morsels for dinner, the fox delivers to his mother the rocky contents of his sack, which, when emptied into the pot of boiling water, cause a splash that scalds both foxes permanently.

You're On!
Ten Steps to a Well-told Tale

1. Begin with drama and end with drama. A crisp, lyrical opening will grab your child's attention. The reason so many tales start out with "once upon a time" is because the phrase instantly thrusts a child into another world, and that is exactly the function of your opening line. Take the child into another reality. Quickly.

   A story about fairy music, arranged by Ruth Sawyer, starts like this:

   > "Here is a tale, how old I can not be telling. It happened long back when fairies were plentiful over Ireland, before the great famine and the plague—which gives a hundred years to it, if it is time that you care anything about."

   Another wonderful opening by Edwin Barrow:

   > "A set of chessmen, left standing on their board, resolved to alter the rules of the game."

   Endings are also important. Many professional storytellers have trademark endings, their own special way of pinching off a tale. "And they lived happily ever after" works, but there are countless other wonderous endings. The Zanzibar Swahili are credited with this ending:

   > "If the story was beautiful, the beauty belongs to all of us; if it was bad, the fault is mine only, who told it."

   Or Hans Christian Andersen's "A Great Grief":

   > "Whoever does not believe this must buy shares from the Tanner's yard."

   The key is to surround your story with eloquence and wit and mystery. The more stories you tell, the more at ease you will be in making this magic.
2. Think of your story "line" as just that: a straight and narrow path from which you must not stray. Tangents are the storyteller's enemy. Woe to him who likes to wander. You will lose all of your dramatic interest if you take your listener off into places and events that have little bearing on your story. The plot is your road map. Use it.
3. Keep descriptions simple and personal. The detail you use in your story ultimately will make it your own. Your objective is to envision your scenery and characters in your mind's eye and to com-

municate what you see. But keep your descriptions spare. Listening is a hard task. Don't go overboard. Make every word count and you will deliver a rich presentation.

4. Prepare, prepare, prepare. Follow the steps for remembering a tale (see page 43) and then practice over and over again. Practice when you take a shower, when you are cooking, or when you are driving. It is better to spend a month preparing a story you can tell for the rest of your life than to spend an afternoon hastily throwing together a tale that will bomb that night and never be told again. Take your time. It truly will pay off.

5. Be patient with your voice. The first time you tell a story you are going to sound a little foolish. Your voice will seem odd and self-conscious, and you might not like it. You can overcome your unsteadiness and awkwardness with practice, *you really can.* In addition, a tape recorder can be an excellent aid for checking weak spots in your story and getting to know your voice. Paradoxically the more seriously you take your storytelling, the more fun and lighthearted your telling will be. Work at it.

6. Maintain eye contact at all times. If you are telling more than one child a story, you can look at the tops of their heads. If you have just one in your audience, look straight into his eyes. Don't be surprised if it is a bit difficult to concentrate when you are staring deep into your favorite pair of eyes. It is at first. But your eye contact is the very thing that will encourage your child to concentrate on the fabulous tale you are about to tell.

7. Speak respectfully to your child. Don't talk down to him, ever. Speak on a one-to-one level, intelligently, enthusiastically. Don't use words that require lots of explanation (on the other hand, a passing explanation can be very effective).

8. If you get lost or forget where you are, stop. Don't proceed until you know exactly where you are going. It doesn't matter how long you stop; what matters is how well you glide back into the tale. When you are ready to resume your telling, simply take a breath and gently reenter. In moments your listeners will have forgotten the interruption completely.

9. Tell stories you like, and be sensitive to the stories your children like. In general, children don't like sentimental, soppy stories, and they don't understand sarcastic stories. So stick to the classics at first; from there you can be aware of which stories you liked to tell and why, as well as those stories that seemed to hit home for your children.

10. Timing is the great trick of storytelling. Work on your pacing, not your decibels. If you want to draw attention to an idea or a word or a phrase, do it by slowing down or pausing or even speeding up. Don't rely on getting louder or softer to make your characters come alive; drama is created through thoughtful timing.

THE THREE LITTLE PIGS

here once was a mother pig who was very poor and had to send her three little pigs out to seek their fortunes.

The first little pig met a man who gave him some straw to build himself a house. He lived happily in the house until a wolf came along and knocked at his door.

"Little pig, little pig, let me come in!" demanded the wolf.

"Not by the hair of my chinny chin chin will I let you in," replied the pig.

"Then I'll huff and I'll puff and I'll blow your house in," said the wolf. So he huffed and he puffed and he blew the house in, and he chased the little pig away.

The second little pig met a man who gave him a bundle of sticks to build himself a house. He lived in the house until the wolf came along and knocked at his door.

"Little pig, little pig, let me come in!" demanded the wolf, and the pig refused, just as his brother had done. The wolf proceeded to huff and to puff and to blow his house in, then chased that little pig away too.

The third little pig met a man who gave him a load of bricks to build himself a house. This little pig built a very fine house and lived in it, just as his brothers had lived in theirs. Eventually the wolf came along and knocked on his door, demanding to be let in. Of course, this little pig refused too. The wolf said he'd huff and puff and blow the house in, but as much as he huffed and puffed, he could not blow the house in.

The wolf rested a few moments, then asked if the little pig would let just the tip of his nose in.

"No," replied the little pig.

The wolf asked if the pig would let his paw in, or the tip of his tail. Each time the pig said, "No."

"Then I'll climb up on your roof and come down through the chimney," threatened the wolf.

The little pig then made a fire so hot, the wolf could not possibly come down the chimney. Finally he went away, and that was the end of the mean old wolf.

The little pig invited his mother to join him, and they both lived happily in their little brick house for many years.

ANNOTATION

In a harder version the first and second pigs are gobbled up by the wolf. The wolf confronts the third pig, who sets the kettle to boil in the fireplace, and the wolf mounts the roof, falls down the chimney, and boils to death. The emphasis is on the laziness of the first two pigs (who built homes of straw and twigs), as contrasted with the industriousness of the third pig, who benefits from his labor.

THE
GINGERBREAD BOY

here once was a woman who had no children of her own. As she wanted one very badly, she decided to bake herself a fine gingerbread boy. She rolled out the dough and cut it in the shape of a little boy with a big smile and plump raisins for eyes. She put the gingerbread boy in the oven, and when she thought he was ready, she opened the oven door. The gingerbread boy hopped off the oven shelf, ran out the kitchen door and down the road.

"Come help me catch the gingerbread boy," the woman called to her husband as she took off after him. When the gingerbread boy saw the woman and the man chasing him, he shouted:

> *"Run, run, as fast as you can,*
> *You can't catch me,*
> *I'm the gingerbread man."*

He soon met a cow who said, "Stop! Stop! I want to eat you." But the gingerbread boy only ran faster than ever, shouting, "I've run away from a woman and a man, and now I'll run away from you!"

And so it was when he met the horse and the farmers in the field, who joined in the chase. In each case he told them whom he'd just escaped from and challenged them with his little verse to catch him.

Eventually he came to a river that he saw no way to cross. The clever fox, who'd had his eye on the gingerbread boy and wanted very much to eat him, saw him hesitate. At last he said politely, "Do you want to cross the river?"

"Yes, please," said the gingerbread boy.

"Just jump on my back, then," said the fox, "and I'll take you across."

All too eagerly the gingerbread boy hopped on the fox's back and followed his instructions about where to sit at each stage of the journey. When they were three quarters of the way across, the fox told the gingerbread boy to climb up onto his head, and so he did. As they drew closer to the opposite shore the fox suggested that the gingerbread boy would be safer if he climbed onto his nose. The gingerbread boy followed all the fox's instructions obediently until he was sitting right across the fox's snout. At that point the fox flipped him in the air and into his open mouth. Two bites and that was the end of the gingerbread boy.

THE EMPEROR'S NEW CLOTHES

here once was an emperor who loved new clothes. He spent a great deal of money on cloaks and doublets and all the things emperors wear. He made a point of never being seen in the same clothes twice.

One day two swindlers presented themselves to the emperor, promising to make him garments of the most exquisite fabric ever woven. The extraordinary feature of these clothes, the swindlers pointed out, is that they become invisible to anyone who is either foolish or unfit for office.

The emperor was easily persuaded to invest in many yards of this wonderful cloth, thinking that the clothes made from it would enable him to tell wise men from fools. From then on, he thought he would know whom he could trust.

The weavers set up their looms and went to work on the new clothes for the emperor. Long into the night, their shuttles flitted back and forth, weaving away with invisible thread. The emperor grew impatient to view his new clothes but was nervous about looking at the cloth, remembering that the weavers had said a fool would not be able to see it. He sent his oldest and wisest minister to see what had been made and report to him. The weavers welcomed the minister's inspection, extolling the colors and the texture and the pattern of the cloth. The minister feared to say that he could not see the cloth. He described the fabric to the emperor in the same glowing terms that it had been described to him.

When the emperor's wife heard how beautiful the new clothes

were, she urged him to wear them in the royal procession the next day.

The following morning, the new clothes were officially presented to the emperor. "Is it not exquisite fabric?" the swindling weavers asked as they flitted about the emperor, making an imaginary tuck here, fastening an invisible clasp there. They spent a great deal of time arranging his royal train before finally pronouncing him ready to appear in public.

News of the emperor's extraordinary raiment had spread far and wide. His subjects were eager to see him dressed in his finery.

As the emperor moved through the crowds in the royal procession, a few people commented on how handsome he looked in his new robes. Other people were silent, not daring to admit that the emperor looked naked to them. At last a child's voice was heard calling out, "But the emperor has nothing on!"

A moment later the crowd echoed the child. "He has nothing on!" they exclaimed, feeling stupid for not having said so before.

The emperor felt more stupid than anyone, for he realized now how he'd been tricked. He knew that he could not rely on his elegant attire to make him look dignified now, so he just held his head high and walked along proudly. His subjects admired him and cheered him more loudly than ever.

THE FISHERMAN AND HIS WIFE

A hardworking fisherman and his wife lived in a humble shack near the sea. Each day the fisherman fished from dawn till dusk. One day, after a long struggle, he landed the biggest flounder he had ever seen. To the fisherman's amazement the flounder could speak, and he asked the fisherman to let him go, explaining that he was no mere flounder but a prince in disguise.

The fisherman agreed to let the flounder go, for he had never met a talking fish before, prince or no prince. He threw back the flounder, went home, and told his wife what had happened. The wife, who was very demanding, berated him for not asking the flounder for wishes, saying that whenever someone does a special favor for a creature with magical powers, they usually are granted several wishes in return. She instructed him to go back to the seashore, find the flounder, and ask for a nice cottage for the couple to live in.

The fisherman did as he was told. Standing on the shore, he called out:

> *"Prince, oh Prince, if such you be*
> *Flounder, flounder in the sea*
> *My faithful wife, Dame Ilsabil,*
> *Has begged a wish against my will."*

The flounder appeared when he was called and told the man that his wish was granted. When the fisherman arrived home, his wife greeted him at the gate of a pleasant little cottage. The fisherman was very pleased, but his wife kept sending him back to the shore to ask more favors. She tired of the cottage and demanded a castle. Then she wanted to be king of all the surrounding land. Next she had to be emperor. And, finally, pope. When her husband thought there was not another thing in the world she could desire, she demanded to be lord of the sun and the moon.

The fisherman returned to the shore once more and summoned the flounder. Reluctantly he told the fish of his wife's latest demand.

This time the wife had gone too far. The flounder informed her husband that he would find her back in their first humble shack when he returned to her. And there the couple remained for the rest of their days.

THE GOLDEN GOOSE

man had three sons, the youngest of whom was named Simpleton. Everyone made fun of him.

One morning the eldest son went into the forest to cut firewood. He took along a sweet cake and a bottle of cider. On the way he met a little old man, who said, "Give me some of your cake and cider, for I am hungry and thirsty."

The young man refused, thinking there would not be enough left over for himself. He set to work chopping down a tree, but almost right away he cut his arm and had to go home. Though this seemed like an accident, it wasn't. The little old man made it happen.

The next day the second son set off into the forest to cut wood and had almost the same experience as his brother. He refused to share his cake and cider with the little old man, and soon after he started chopping down a tree, he cut his leg and had to go home.

Against his father's advice, Simpleton set out to chop some wood. He took with him a bottle of stale cider and some cake that had been baked in the ashes. When he met the little old man, he agreed to share his cake and cider, which became sweet and tasty as they ate.

The old man rewarded Simpleton for his kindness by instructing him to chop down an old tree that had a goose with golden feathers in its trunk. Simpleton took the goose to an inn where he planned to spend the night.

The landlord of the inn had three daughters. Each one wanted to pluck out one of the goose's golden feathers. When the first one tried, she stuck to the goose. When each daughter tried to pluck a feather, she stuck to her sister. They all spent the night stuck together, and in the morning Simpleton picked up the goose and walked off. Everyone they passed as they went along stuck to the person he or she touched in this strange entourage.

After a while they came to the town where the king lived. This king had a daughter who appeared not to know how to laugh. The king had let it be known that anyone who could make his daughter laugh could marry her. When Simpleton and his group passed beneath her window in the palace, the daughter laughed uproariously.

The king was not especially pleased about having a son named Simpleton, so he set all kinds of tasks for him to do before he could marry his daughter. Simpleton first was told to find a man who could drink all of the cider in the king's cellar. He went to the forest, not knowing what to do, and suddenly encountered the little old man who had given him the golden goose. The old man claimed he was dying of thirst. Back to the king's cellar the twosome went, and the old man drank all of the cider. The king, flustered, then challenged Simpleton to find someone who could eat a mountain of bread. Simpleton went back to the forest, recruiting the old man to eat and eat and eat. The king's final order was to find a ship that could sail on land as well as in water. Nearly beaten, Simpleton headed to the forest where he sat down next to the little old man.

"I have drunk all the cider in the king's cellar," the old man said, "and I have eaten a mountain of bread. I will give you the ship you need to please the king, because of your kindness to me."

The little old man kept his promise, and Simpleton was able to marry the king's daughter. He and the princess lived together happily for many years, and when the king died, Simpleton ruled his entire kingdom.

LITTLE RED RIDING HOOD

here once was a sweet little girl who was loved by all who knew her. Her grandmother was particularly fond of her and had made her a pretty red cape with a hood, which the child always wore, and so she became known as Little Red Riding Hood.

One morning Little Red Riding Hood's mother packed a basket of cakes and butter and asked Red Riding Hood to take it to her grandmother, who was ill in bed. Little Red Riding Hood set out along a path through the woods to her grandmother's house some distance away.

She had not gone far when she met a wolf who greeted her politely. "Where are you going on this beautiful day?" he inquired, thinking, while she answered, that he would like to eat her up.

"Why don't you pick some pretty flowers to take to your grandmother?" the wolf suggested, already planning to get to Little Red Riding Hood's grandmother's house before her. As Little Red Riding Hood lingered among the flowers, the wolf ran to Grandmother's house, gulped her down, put on her nightgown and cap, and climbed under the covers.

Soon Little Red Riding Hood ran along to her grandmother's house and, finding the door ajar, let herself in.

"Good morning, Grandmother," she called out, thinking to herself that Grandmother looked a little strange today.

"Oh, Grandmother, what big ears you have!" she exclaimed, wondering why she had never noticed them before.

"The better to hear you with, my dear," said the wolf, who was lying there dressed up as Grandmother.

"And what big eyes you have!"

"The better to see you with, my dear," said the wolf, leering hungrily.

"Oh, Grandmother, what big *teeth* you have!"

"The better to eat you with!" said the wolf, and he leapt from the bed and gobbled Little Red Riding Hood all up.

Just at that moment a woodsman was passing by Grandmother's house and decided to look in and see how she was. When he saw the wolf asleep in Grandmother's bed, he figured something terrible had happened. He killed the wolf with one blow of his ax, then cut him open. As soon as he did so, out stepped Little Red Riding Hood and Grandmother.

They were very grateful to the woodsman for saving them and invited him to share the cakes and butter Little Red Riding Hood had brought for Grandmother.

Hans Christian Andersen

The statue built in his honor in Copenhagen bears the inscription, "H. C. Andersen, Digter." Translated from Danish, the word *digter* means a mixture of poet and writer. Hans Christian Andersen was a novelist as well as a poet and teller of fairy tales. He was highly regarded by other writers, scholars, storytellers, and he was beloved by children.

Andersen was born in Odense, Denmark, in 1805. His father was a shoemaker; his mother a washerwoman. Hans's father read endlessly to his son, and his mother taught him everything she knew about Danish folklore. Though the Andersens had little money and few possessions, Hans lived in a world of fantasy that gave him endless delight.

When he was only fourteen, Hans, who had never gone to school, left Odense to go to Copenhagen. He aspired to a career in acting, thinking that the opportunity to play many roles would give him outlets for his lively imagination. But tall, gangling Hans was not well suited to many parts. However, his oafish charm won him many friends who read his poetry and encouraged his efforts in that direction. When Hans was about seventeen, some of these friends persuaded him to accept a grant as a student: He had never attended elementary school, and all he knew, including reading and writing, was self-taught. His friends convinced him that he must start from the beginning—first grade. He must have been an unlikely-looking member of that class, tall as he was, and with hands and feet that did not seem to be related to the rest of his body. But Hans persevered, grade by grade, until he eventually received his university degree. Then he felt free to write.

Perhaps because of his years as an ungainly schoolboy, Hans Christian Andersen always regarded himself as different from other people. Many of the stories he wrote reflect that sense of loneliness. "The Ugly Duckling" reveals his understanding of what it is like to feel different from others. Through "The Little Mermaid" Andersen again expresses the great loneliness one can feel even when surrounded by kind people.

Andersen seemed to lose his feeling of alienation when he was with children. He knew a thousand ways to entertain them, with stories, poems, games, and his own inimitable antics. When he was about thirty years old, in a desperate attempt to earn money, he gathered four of the tales children most enjoyed hearing into a volume for publication. These were probably stories he had learned as a child, closely related to the folklore his mother had shared with him. The book was so successful that he published a volume almost every year thereafter, soon moving from the folktales of his youth to stories entirely of his own creation. These were enthusiastically received and passed around the world. Andersen's tales are now available in eighty languages, including Chinese, Hindustani, Swahili, and Esperanto.

Andersen died when he was seventy years old at the summer villa of a friend. His grave is in Copenhagen, but his devoted readers usually visit his statue in the King's Garden or the figure of the Little Mermaid in Langeline. Others travel to Odense to see the house where he was born, kept as it was over one hundred years ago when he lived there.

THE UGLY DUCKLING

One particularly beautiful summer day a mother duck sat among the reeds of a little pond, hatching her brood of ducklings. The last one was taking a long time to hatch. Finally the egg opened and out tumbled the baby. He looked nothing like his brothers and sisters. He was big for a duckling, gray instead of yellow, and just plain ugly. His mother thought perhaps he was a turkey chick but found, to her amazement, that he swam as well as any of her other children.

When the mother duck took the ducklings to the farmyard, the other animals made fun of the ugly duckling and commented on his strange looks. Even after the other ducklings adjusted to life in the farmyard, the ugly duckling was insulted and teased by everyone. Finally he couldn't take it any longer. He made up his mind to run away.

That night he stayed in a marsh where some wild ducks lived. In the morning, when they saw him, they said they thought he was so ugly that they liked him. They invited him to stay with them. Just at that moment two hunters' shots rang out, and a big hunting dog came splashing into the swamp. The dog gave the duckling a curious sniff, then splashed on by. The duckling was sure that because he was so ugly, even the dog wouldn't touch him.

The duckling wandered on until he came to a miserable little cottage with a light on inside. It seemed that an old woman lived there with her cat and a hen. The duckling had hoped to linger awhile there, but the cat and the hen thought he was so ugly, they didn't want him in the house. When the old woman found out he could not lay eggs, she didn't want him around, either.

Soon autumn came. The leaves began to flutter from the trees and it grew colder. The poor duckling was very unhappy. One evening he saw some birds flying south. He thought they were the most beautiful, graceful creatures he had ever seen. The duckling found a lake to swim in, but as winter came, the circle of water that the duckling had to swim in grew smaller and smaller. Finally the ice closed in and he had no place to swim. A farmer saw him, broke the ice to release him, and took the duckling home to his family. The children wanted to play with him, but they were rough and frightened the duckling. He flew into the flour barrel, creating a cloud of flour, and nearly got stuck in the butter tub. The children screeched with laughter, and the wife, at her wit's end, chased him out of the house. He found his way to the woods where he sheltered himself as best he could through the long, cold winter.

When spring came, the duckling flapped his wings and flew up into the sky. Riding the wind, he saw three swans, as beautiful as any creatures he had ever seen. He felt a tremendous impulse to join them, even though he thought they might peck him to death because he was ugly. He decided that he wanted to be with them no matter what. He flew down to the water and swam toward the swans. As he did so, he caught sight of his reflection in the water. He could not believe his eyes. His neck was curved and graceful. His wings were thick with white feathers. He was a swan. The other swans welcomed him as one of them. "Look, a new brother! And the most beautiful of all," they said. He had not the courage to tell them that he had never dreamed of such happiness when he was an ugly duckling.

JACK AND THE BEANSTALK

here once was a widow who was very poor. All she had in the world was her son named Jack and an old cow named Milky Way. They depended on the cow to give milk for them to sell at market. But one day Milky Way stopped giving milk completely. Jack and his mother decided that he would sell Milky Way for as much as he could get for her.

On his way to market Jack met a strange man who seemed very friendly. "Do you know how many beans make five?" he asked Jack. As quick as lightning, Jack replied to the riddle, "Two in each hand and one in my mouth!"

Complimenting Jack on his quickness, the man pulled five beans out of his pocket and offered them to Jack, saying they were magic beans that would produce a stalk that would grow right up to the sky. He said he would take Milky Way in exchange for the beans. It seemed like a good deal to Jack, but he had trouble explaining to his mother what he'd done when he arrived home. She scolded him for his foolishness, sent him to bed without any supper, and cast the beans outside the window in disgust.

The next day, when Jack woke up, there was a huge beanstalk growing outside his window. It grew right up to the sky. Jack hopped onto it from his bedroom window and climbed and climbed until he reached the sky. At the top he found a long, winding road leading to a very big house. On the doorstep was an immensely large woman. Jack greeted her and asked politely if she could give him some breakfast. She replied that he'd better be careful that her husband the giant ogre didn't make breakfast out of *him*, as he loved little boys broiled on toast. Just as the woman was sneaking some bread and cheese to Jack, there was a great *thump-thump*, indicating that the ogre was on his way. His wife scuttled Jack into the oven in the nick of time. "What do I smell?" he shouted. Then:

> *"Fee-fi-fo-fum*
> *I smell the blood of an Englishman!*
> *Be he alive, or be he dead,*
> *I'll have his bones to grind my bread."*

After breakfast the giant took out his bags of gold. He counted his gold coins until he began to yawn, then finally he nodded off to sleep. Slowly Jack crept out of the oven and past the ogre, grabbing a bag of gold as he went. He ran along quickly to the beanstalk, dropped the bag down into his mother's garden, then climbed down after it himself.

Jack and his mother supported themselves with the ogre's gold for some time, but finally it ran out. Jack climbed the beanstalk again, and this time, after a close brush with the ogre, he came back with a hen that laid golden eggs. By selling these, Jack and his mother were able to live comfortably, but Jack grew restless and mounted the beanstalk once more. This time he sneaked into the ogre's house and, after hiding in the copper pot, was just making off with the ogre's singing harp when the ogre saw him and followed him down the road. Jack swung himself onto the beanstalk with the harp, which cried out "Master! Master!" to the ogre not far behind him. Once on the ground, Jack asked his mother for an ax, which he used to give the beanstalk a good whack. One more whack brought the giant tumbling to his doom.

Jack and his mother grew rich by selling the golden eggs and displaying the singing harp. It is said that Jack eventually married a beautiful princess, and all lived happily ever after.

SNOW WHITE
AND ROSE RED

 widow lived in a modest cottage with her daughters Snow White and Rose Red, who were as beautiful as the flowers on two rosebushes that grew by the cottage door. The daughters were also blessed with virtue and good fortune, and wherever they went, no harm ever came to them.

One evening a large black bear knocked on their door. The young girls were frightened by the sight of him, but he said he was freezing to death and only wanted to warm himself by the fire. The widow felt sorry for him and invited him in. She and her daughters fussed over the bear, making him comfortable until even the lamb and the dove who lived with the family were not afraid.

The bear stayed the night with the family, then went on his way in the snow. He came back every evening to visit and let the children play with him. But when spring came, he announced that he would not be coming back for a while as he had to go deep into the forest to protect his treasures from the evil dwarfs. Snow White was so reluctant to let him go that the bear had to squeeze out the door, leaving a piece of his hairy coat on the latch. Snow White thought she glimpsed gold glittering beneath the fur, but she wasn't sure.

Soon afterward, while gathering sticks in the woods, the widow's daughters encountered a crabby old dwarf with his beard caught in a half-split tree. The children tried to help, and after tugging away at the beard to no avail, Snow White whipped out her scissors and snipped off the end of the dwarf's beard. The ungrateful dwarf merely grumbled that they had cut off his beautiful beard and, cursing them roundly, marched off.

Not long afterward the maidens met the dwarf again, this time with his beard caught in his own fishing line. Once again the daughters tried to release him, and again they resorted to snipping off a bit of beard to do so. "You fool!" he raged at Snow White. "Do you want to totally disfigure me?" He muttered another curse upon them, then took up a bag of pearls that appeared to belong to him and slipped behind a stone.

A few days later the girls were doing an errand for their mother when they saw an eagle swoop down out of the air, dip behind a rock, and reappear with the crabby old dwarf in his beak. The virtuous girls again came to his rescue, only to be criticized mercilessly for not being more gentle about it. With that the dwarf went off to his cave with a bagful of precious stones.

On their way home the maidens came upon the dwarf with his treasures spread out about him in the sun. Enraged to be caught with his stolen booty, the dwarf ranted and raved at the girls more loudly than ever before. In the middle of this a large black bear emerged from the forest and came roaring toward the dwarf, who begged for his life and urged the bear to have the two girls to eat instead, as they would make a tastier meal than he would.

The bear made short work of the dwarf with his enormous paw. As the girls ran off in fright a voice called after them, "Snow White, Rose Red. Don't be afraid. Wait for me." They turned to see a handsome young man all dressed in gold. He explained that he was a prince who had been condemned by the wicked dwarf to live as a bear until the dwarf's death broke the spell.

In due course Snow White was married to the prince and Rose Red to his equally handsome brother. The two couples shared the treasures the dwarf had collected. The widow lived with them in the palace. The rosebushes that had stood by the cottage were planted before the palace, and every year beautiful red and white roses bloomed in profusion.

HANSEL AND GRETEL

here once was a woodcutter who lived close to a very large forest with his wife and two children. The boy was called Hansel and the girl Gretel. They had always been poor, but when a famine struck the land, there was not enough food for the whole family.

The woodcutter simply could not think of a way to make ends meet. His wife, who was the children's stepmother, suggested that they take the children into the forest, light a fire, and give them each a piece of bread. "Then," she said, "we'll go about our work and leave them there. They'll be lost and we'll be rid of them forever."

The woodcutter was reluctant to abandon his children, but his wife called him a fool and gave him no peace until he consented.

The children, too hungry to sleep, overheard their stepmother. Gretel began to cry bitterly. Hansel consoled her, promising to find a way to save them.

When the woodcutter and his wife were asleep, Hansel opened the door and slipped out. The white pebbles around the house shone like silver buttons in the moonlight. Hansel gathered as many of them as his pockets would hold.

Even before the sun had risen, the stepmother woke the children, telling them they were all going into the forest to fetch wood. She gave them each a piece of bread for their dinner, warning them not to eat it too fast, as they would not get more. Gretel put the bread in her pocket.

As they walked along, Hansel kept turning around, and each time he did, he dropped a white pebble on the ground.

In the middle of the forest their father made a fire to keep them warm. The stepmother told them to rest themselves while she and her husband went to cut wood. She said they would come back later to fetch them. Hansel and Gretel sat by the fire and ate their piece of bread. At last they fell fast asleep.

When they awoke, it was very dark. Gretel was frightened, but Hansel told her that when the moon rose, they would be able to find their way.

A little later Hansel took his sister's hand, and guided by the pebbles that glittered like silver buttons in the moonlight, they found their way back to their father's cottage.

Not long afterward the children once again heard their step-mother plotting to leave them in the woods. This time Hansel was unable to gather pebbles, as his stepmother had locked the door and he couldn't go outside. The next morning, when the children were given their bread, Hansel crumbled his in his pocket and dropped the crumbs on the ground as they walked along.

When they were deep in the forest, their father again made a big fire. The stepmother told the children to rest themselves while she and her husband fetched more wood. Gretel shared her bread with Hansel and they fell asleep. When they awoke, they were saddened to find that birds had eaten all the bread crumbs, and they could not find their way out of the forest.

The next morning they started to walk but had no idea where they were going. Suddenly they caught sight of a beautiful golden bird that sang very sweetly and seemed to want the children to follow it. It led them to a little cottage that appeared to be made out of candy and cake. To their amazement it really was, and the children were so hungry that they didn't hesitate to nibble at it. Just as they were breaking off a piece of the roof to see what it tasted like, a gentle voice called out to them and asked who was there.

But before they could answer, the door of the little house opened and an old, old woman, supporting herself with a cane, came hobbling out. Hansel and Gretel were so frightened that they dropped their food.

But the old woman was very nice to them. She led them inside the little house where they found a fine dinner of things children love to eat waiting for them. After they'd eaten, she showed them two little beds prepared just for them. They crept beneath the blankets and fell sound asleep.

The old woman who seemed so kind was really a witch. She had built her house of candy and cake to lure children to her, and then she cooked them and ate them as a special treat. She gazed at Hansel and Gretel in their beds, thinking they would make tasty morsels.

The next morning she took Hansel and put him in the barn and locked the door. She forced Gretel to cook for him so he would get fattened up. Each day the witch felt Hansel's finger to see how fat he was. But the witch's eyes were dim, and Hansel gave her only his knuckle to feel, so the witch didn't think he'd made much progress.

One day she grew impatient and told Gretel to fetch the water to boil him. The witch was going to eat him, fat or thin.

The next morning, as Gretel was forced to fill the kettle and kindle the fire, the witch announced that she intended to bake first. "I think I'll bake some bread now. Creep in," she said to Gretel, "and see if the oven is hot enough."

She meant to push Gretel in and roast her, and Gretel knew it. She pretended she didn't know how to get into the oven and asked the witch to show her.

"Silly child!" cried the witch. "The opening is more than adequate. See, I could fit in it myself."

Gretel gave the witch an enormous push that sent her all the way in. Then she slammed the door and bolted it. Gretel ran to the stable to let Hansel out, crying, "Hansel, do not fear! The wicked witch is dead."

As soon as the door was opened, Hansel sprang out of the barn and threw his arms around his sister. They went into the witch's house where they found treasures beyond belief. They filled their pockets with as much as they could carry before they set about finding a way out of the woods.

They had not gone far when they came to a large body of water. Just as they were wondering how to cross it, Gretel spotted a duck swimming. She implored the duck to help, and her wish was granted as the duck swam over to them and carried Hansel and Gretel across the water, one child at a time.

On the opposite shore the woods seemed more familiar to them and they gradually found their way to their father's cottage. He welcomed them warmly, telling them that he had missed them desperately and that while they were away their stepmother had died. The children shared their treasures with their father, knowing that their troubles were ended. From then on the family lived together in love and prosperity.

What Happens Next?
Keeping Your Plots Straight

The first step to remembering a story is choosing it well. Ruth Sawyer, one of the most accomplished twentieth-century storytellers, emphasizes the importance of the selection process with a caveat. The power of proper selection, she warns, is not just having a preference for a story but almost an instinct for it. The instinct for this story almost transcends the issue of whether you like it or not. As beginners, we are safe in confining our selections to simple tales that are tightly organized and fun.

Presumably you have read your tale once for pleasure. Now go back and read it for "visuals." As you read it, visualize the characters, the settings, the movement from scene to scene. Make it a silent movie you are seeing in your mind's eye for the first time. Concentrate.

Now, for your third reading, break up your silent movie into scenes or incidents. You might even want to write them down (I do). If, for example, you are working on "Little Red Riding Hood," you might have a sequence like this: 1) Red sets out to deliver cake and butter; 2) wolf sidetracks; 3) wolf to Grandma's, eats her; 4) Red encounters wolf in Grandma's clothes; 5) Wolf eats Red; 6) woodsman; 7) three eat cake.

This technique of fixing incidents in your memory is the key to effective remembering.

For your fourth reading, add "sound." This time you will study key phrases and dialogue and important descriptions. Tie the sound to the visuals. *Your words must communicate the images you have in your mind.* As you run through your story you will hear the rhythm and mood. Its pace will become apparent. Many serious storytellers working with exquisite original versions memorize the entire work, word for word. For the casual teller the basics will do, but down the road you might want to experiment with beautifully worded story versions and memorize them for your children.

At this point you have read the story once and have "seen the movie" three times. Read through your story once more and pretend you are there, watching this amazing tale unfold, hiding behind a tree or an overstuffed chair. Brand this experience into your memory. You were there. It should now be a real experience, one you witnessed firsthand.

If you like, you can pause now, for a day or so, and let the story sit awhile.

When you are ready, you can practice telling your story for the first time. Your voice will be awkward at first, and you will have weak spots here and there; don't be concerned. Be simple and precise. The story is yours. And the more you tell your story, the more you will see that the story has a life of its own, a life that will carry you through each telling.

BEAUTY AND THE BEAST

rich merchant had three daughters, one of whom was particularly lovely and was called Beauty. Though they had all lived well for many years, one day things changed for the merchant and he lost everything he owned. All he had left was a small country cottage where he went to live with his daughters. The two older daughters were lazy and complained bitterly about their lost riches while Beauty did most of the work and tried hard to make her father happy.

One morning the merchant received news that one of his ships, which he thought was lost, had arrived safely in port. He felt sure that if he went to the ship, he could recover some of the fortune he thought he'd lost. He asked his daughters what presents they wanted him to bring back. The two eldest mentioned all kinds of finery; Beauty wanted only a rose.

When the merchant reached the port where the ship had docked, he found that his partners, believing him dead, had divided the ship's contents among themselves. The merchant was obliged to turn back without anything to show for his efforts.

The way home led through a dense forest where the snow was so deep, the merchant's horse could hardly move. Just when the merchant was about to give up in despair, he caught sight of a light shining through the trees. He discovered that it came from a great castle that seemed to be quite empty, though a table was set in a small sitting room and a fire blazed cozily in the hearth. The merchant helped himself to the meal on the table, as it seemed to have been prepared for him. He fell asleep by the fire and in the morning awoke early, eager to find his host and thank him. In his search he came to a garden with roses blooming. Remembering Beauty's request, he plucked one to take to her. At that moment a hideous beast appeared, accusing the merchant of stealing his roses. "For this you must die!" he declared.

The poor merchant fell to his knees and tried to explain that he had picked the rose only because he had promised his youngest daughter that he would bring her one. When the Beast heard this, he answered, "I will allow you to go if you send one of your daughters to take your place. She must come willingly, or you yourself will have to return within three months."

The merchant returned to his cottage and related to his daughters what the Beast had said. The two older daughters blamed Beauty for causing all the trouble. But Beauty said without hesitation that she would go to the Beast's castle in place of her father.

Three months later Beauty and her father traveled to the Beast's castle where she explained to him that she had come willingly. The merchant left the next morning, and Beauty found herself surrounded by treasures galore. Everything was arranged for her comfort and enjoyment. At dinnertime each night the Beast would visit her. He was very gentle and kind, but each time he came, he would ask her to marry him. Beauty always said no.

After a while Beauty began to miss her father and worry about him. She asked the Beast's permission to let her go home. He agreed, on the condition that she return in eight days. He said that if she did not return, he would die. He gave her a magic ring that would take her to her father, then return her to the Beast's castle.

Beauty's family was delighted to see her, though her sisters were jealous of her life in the castle. When the week with them was over, they tried to trick Beauty into staying longer. Beauty lingered a while, but one night she had a dream that the Beast was dying. Beauty quickly found the magic ring and rubbed it as the Beast had instructed her to do. Almost instantly she was back at the castle where she found the Beast lying in the garden. He appeared to be dead, and Beauty felt it was her fault for not having returned sooner. Then he opened his eyes, and she saw that he was just barely alive.

"Dear Beast, you must not die," she cried. "You must live and be my beloved husband."

At that moment the castle began to glow with light, and a handsome prince stood beside Beauty. He explained that her words had broken a magic spell that had forced him to take the form of a beast. The spell could be broken only when someone loved him in spite of his ugliness.

The prince and Beauty were married the next day, and her family was sent for to join in the celebration.

THE SLEEPING BEAUTY

here once lived a king and queen who were bitterly unhappy because they could have no children. But after a great many years, as if by a miracle, the queen gave birth to a baby daughter. Seven fairies were asked to be godmothers to the child, and plans were made for a magnificent christening at which each would give the princess a gift of talent or beauty or virtue that would insure her happiness and good fortune.

After the christening ceremony a great banquet was held in honor of all the fairies. At each of their places the king had set gifts of gold and precious jewels. Just as everyone was sitting down at the table, a very old fairy entered the hall. The king had not invited her because she had not been seen for more than fifty years and everyone thought she was dead. The king ordered that a place be set for her at the table, but he did not have gold and jewels for her as he did for the others. The old fairy regarded this as a great slight, and she began to mumble threats and curses under her breath.

One of the young fairies who sat nearby began to worry that the old fairy would cause some harm to befall the infant princess. As the other fairies were making their gifts to the princess, the young fairy hid behind a curtain, hoping to be the last to make a gift, so that she could undo whatever evil the old fairy might wish upon the princess. After the other fairies had made their gifts of grace and musical ability and beauty beyond compare, the old fairy stepped forward to take her turn. Quivering with rage and spite, she declared that the princess would prick her finger on a spindle and die. The guests were struck dumb with horror until the last fairy, who had been hiding behind the curtain, cried out, "No, Your Majesties. The princess will not die of this wound." She explained that she did not have the power to totally undo an older fairy's wish, but she could alter it so that the princess would only fall into a deep sleep. The princess would sleep a hundred years and be awakened at the end of that time by a king's son.

In a desperate attempt to prevent either prophecy from being fulfilled, the king ordered all spindles removed from his kingdom. Anyone found using a spinning wheel was to be put to death.

One day when the princess was about fifteen, the king and queen were away from the castle for the day. The princess was amusing herself by exploring the castle. At the top of a tower she came upon an old woman servant using a spindle. She had never heard of the king's edict against them. The princess was fascinated and wanted to try her hand at spinning. No sooner had she touched the spindle than she pricked her finger and fell to the floor in a swoon. Nothing the old woman or any of the servants and courtiers could do would revive the young girl.

When they returned, the king and queen saw that their worst fears had been realized. The princess was carried into the most beautiful room in the castle and laid upon a bed with elegantly embroidered coverings. There she was left to sleep in peace.

The good fairy who had changed the old fairy's wicked curse heard the news of what had happened and hastened to the palace in a fiery chariot drawn by dragons. She touched all the people who worked in the castle with her magic wand, as well as the princess's little dog Puff, causing them to fall asleep with the princess. Then the king and queen left the castle, and a vast forest of trees grew up around the castle.

A hundred years later the son of a king was hunting in the countryside around the castle. He inquired about the thick hedges and trees that surrounded it, was told the story of the sleeping princess, and decided that he would be the one to awaken her. He made his way to the castle and found the rooms crowded with sleeping people. At last he came to the princess, as beautiful as she had been when she fell asleep. As he gazed at her the princess awoke. "Is it you, my prince?" she said. "You have been so long in coming!"

The prince and princess were enchanted with each other. It seemed as if, in her slumbers, the princess had dreamed of the moment of meeting her prince and was eager to get to know him. They talked for hours, then dined on a supper prepared by the lady-in-waiting who, with the rest of the palace staff, had fully awakened by now.

They were married after supper in the palace chapel and the next morning traveled to the city ruled by the prince's father where they were welcomed warmly.

ANNOTATION

In the Perrault version of "The Sleeping Beauty," the prince leaves his bride after the wedding and returns to his parents' castle. He does not tell them of his marriage for two years but continues to sneak away to see the princess in the forest. Two children are born, whom the prince hesitates to introduce to his mother even after the public announcement of his marriage following the king's death. It is rumored that the queen mother had ogreish tendencies, which, soon after meeting her grandchildren, she demonstrated by ordering the chief steward of the castle to serve first one grandchild and then the other for her dinner. The steward manages to protect the children and their mother from the ogre, who eventually ends up in a vat of poisonous brew that she had prepared for her grandchildren and their mother. Then, at last, the king and his family lived in peace.

The somewhat more widely known version of "The Sleeping Beauty" by the Brothers Grimm features thirteen fairies, including the evil one. The princess is called Briar Rose, and when she falls asleep, the king and queen sleep with her. The prince awakens her with a kiss, and as he does so, the evil fairy's spell is broken and everyone in the castle awakens to celebrate together. The prince and Briar Rose are married a few days later and live happily "in peace and joy until they die."

Charles Perrault

Charles Perrault was a learned Frenchman who enjoyed the honor of membership in the French Academy under King Louis XIV. His older brother, Claude Perrault, was a scientist and architect, best known for his work on the Louvre in Paris.

Charles Perrault became very involved in a major literary battle of the late seventeenth century called the Quarrel of the Ancients and the Moderns. He and his supporters took the position that the culture of his time was superior to that of ancient Greece and Rome. Perrault's thoughts were expressed dramatically in a poem written in 1687, in which he compared ancient authors unfavorably with contemporary writers. The poem inspired Boileau, primary defender of the "Ancients," to trade insults with Perrault for several years thereafter.

In spite of his many scholarly treatises, Perrault is best remembered for the small volume of fairy tales he had published under his ten-year-old son's name in 1697. These tales were collected by Perrault and rewritten for the amusement of the French Court and be-

came popular with children as well. The book was called *Histoires ou contes du temps passé (Stories or Tales of Olden Times)* and included such classic tales as "The Sleeping Beauty," "Little Red Riding Hood," "Bluebeard," "Cinderella," and "Tom Thumb." In the frontispiece of the collection he refers to the stories as *"Contes de ma mère l'oye,"* tales of Mother Goose. Perrault offers no explanation of who she is.

Though Perrault technically was not the author of the stories in his collection, his tales bear the indisputable mark of his way of telling them. He does not hesitate to dwell on gruesome details, such as the slaying of the seven little ogresses in "Tom Thumb," nor does he refrain from lacing his stories with wry comments about the paradoxes of human nature. And, unlike most tellers of fairy tales, he sometimes gives in to the impulse to bend his subject matter at the end to bring it to the conclusion he wants the story to have: the "morals" Perrault added to his tales were a source of great amusement to the adults who heard them and were usually omitted in telling the stories to children.

CINDERELLA

here once was a man who married a proud and haughty woman after his first wife died. She had two daughters exactly like herself. The husband had a daughter who was as beautiful and gentle as her mother had been.

The stepmother forced her husband's daughter to do all the housework and to wait upon her and her daughters night and day. Whenever she had a moment, the hardworking child would sit quietly in the chimney corner among the cinders. And so her stepsisters came to call her Cinderwench, or sometimes Cinderella.

One day it was announced that the king's son would give a series of balls for the fashionable people of the realm. Cinderella's two sisters were invited and immediately started planning what they would wear. To make Cinderella envious the sisters asked her if she wouldn't like to go to the ball. She answered, saying that she couldn't even dream of such a thing.

On the evening of the ball Cinderella helped her sisters dress and fix their hair. When they left, she sat down by the fire and cried.

Instantly her fairy godmother appeared and asked her why she was so unhappy.

"I wish, I wish I could . . ."

"I know," said the fairy godmother. "You want to go to the ball, and so you shall."

Cinderella was instructed to find a pumpkin in the garden. She did so, and when her fairy godmother touched it with her wand, it turned into a golden coach. The godmother sent her to find six live mice, and these were turned into a set of fine horses to draw the coach. The fairy godmother selected from the rattrap the rat with the longest whiskers, to be transformed into a fine, fat coachman to drive the golden coach. Six lizards were brought from the garden by their tails, to become six footmen dressed in livery who jumped up behind the coach just as footmen are meant to do.

It seemed Cinderella was all set to go to the ball, except for her raggedy clothes. With one touch of her fairy godmother's wand these were turned into a gown of gold and silver, embroidered with jewels. For Cinderella's feet there were the prettiest glass slippers ever worn by any princess. Just as Cinderella was mounting her coach, the fairy godmother warned her that she must return by midnight, otherwise her coach would become a pumpkin, her horses mice, her coachman a rat, her footmen lizards, and her clothing nothing but rags.

Cinderella promised she would not be late and set off to the ball quite dizzy with happiness.

For some mysterious reason the king's son seemed to be waiting for her at the palace. He did not let her out of his sight the entire evening. Everyone at the ball was completely dazzled by the loveliness of the unknown princess. Her sisters were quite overwhelmed by her kindnesses to them, though they did not recognize her. When Cinderella heard the clock begin to strike twelve, she graciously bid everyone good night and went off in her golden coach, which delivered her safely to her door.

At home she found her fairy godmother pleased that she had come back on time. Cinderella thanked her and asked if she could go to the ball the following night.

The two sisters returned full of descriptions of the mysterious princess. Cinderella asked many questions about her, then begged the eldest sister to let her borrow her dress so that she might attend the ball and see the beautiful princess. The sister refused, as Cinderella expected she would.

The next night the two sisters went off to the ball, and Cinderella followed shortly afterward, more exquisitely attired than she had been the night before. Once again the king's son was captivated by her. Cinderella herself was so entranced that she lost track of the time until she heard the clock begin to strike twelve. She leapt up immediately and fled. The prince ran after her, but she vanished almost immediately, leaving behind one glass slipper. The prince retrieved this and took it with him.

Cinderella's coach had disappeared, and she had to run home through the streets in her ragged clothes. Her sisters talked endlessly of the ball and the mysterious disappearance of the unknown princess.

A few days later the king's son announced that he would marry the woman whose delicate foot the shoe fitted. A courtier took the shoe from house to house, and all the marriageable young ladies tried it on. Finally it was brought to Cinderella's sisters and they tried it on. It was much too tight for either of them.

"Let me try it on," Cinderella said gently. Her sisters mocked her, but the courtier carried out his orders to try it on every woman in the realm. Of course, it slid on easily. Cinderella then took from her skirt pocket the other tiny slipper and put it on. Instantly her godmother's magic spell was upon her and Cinderella was transformed into the beautiful, elegantly dressed lady she had been at the ball.

Her sisters recognized her as the unknown princess and begged her pardon for all their former unkindness. Cinderella forgave them and said she hoped they would love her always.

Cinderella was taken by the courtier to the palace where the prince vowed he would love her forever and asked for the wedding to be arranged immediately. Cinderella invited her sisters to live in the palace, and not long afterward they were married to two lords of the court.

The Pregnant Pause and Other Tricks of the Teller's Trade

This is a book about voices, whether they are weaving a tale or singing a lullaby. Meeting your voice for the first time can be an odd experience, something akin to looking at your back straight on. But you should confront your voice—for better or worse—and prime it for the storytelling journey. When you do, here are a few things to consider:

- As a beginner, you shouldn't change your voice too much for each character. You are not supposed to be acting, you are supposed to be recounting what happened. New storytellers often make the mistake of overacting, and it really distracts their audiences. Use inflection to soften your female voice and to deepen your male voice. If your child is three or older, don't make a big to-do about animals; don't cluck and howl and peep alot. Animals are usually personifications of people we all know, and they should speak as such.

- The greatest challenge for me was to wipe out all of those *ers*, *ums*, *you knows*, and *ahs* from my presentation. (And I'm still trying.) But it is easier than you think if you truly concentrate on what you are saying. If you get lost, just pause and focus mentally on where you are and where

you are going. Don't panic; your child has no doubt forgiven you for worse.

- Pacing is a key factor. It is also an art that can be mastered with practice. Your sense of pacing is a natural instinct, and I can prove it to you. Pick up a favorite novel and read a page or two aloud. Notice how you pick up your pace when there is a lot of movement and action and how you slow down for the descriptive passages. This is exactly how you will tell your story, and your pacing will build in dramatic interest. Action words come off easily. Description needs more attention (which is why you should avoid too much of it). When you tell a story, be aware of how much drama you can add with thoughtful pacing.

- The pause is the most powerful technique you can use to create drama, suspense, and interest in your story. A well-placed pause can rivet your audience. An example: "He limped to the door. There [pause] was Barbara." Compare that to: "He limped to the door. There was Barbara." Obviously you can use this technique too much, so be judicious. But don't forget how much power it will add to your telling.

THUMBELINA

here was once a woman who wanted a child so much that she sought the advice of a witch. The witch, who was accustomed to the problem, gave the woman a magic seed and instructed her to plant it in a flowerpot with lots of rich soil. The woman watered it faithfully, and soon a flower began to grow. One day the woman kissed the bud that had begun to form, and when she did, it opened its petals to reveal a beautiful little girl no bigger than her thumb. The woman named her Thumbelina.

Thumbelina never grew any bigger. She slept in a walnut shell beneath fresh flower petals. In the daytime she often sang in the sunlight with a sweet, haunting voice.

One night an ugly toad found her way into Thumbelina's room and saw her sleeping in the walnut shell. "There's the perfect wife for my son," she croaked, and whisked Thumbelina away, walnut shell and all. Some time later Thumbelina awoke on a water lily in the middle of a pond and was introduced by the old toad to her son who, Thumbelina was told, would soon be her husband. Thumbelina was frightened, but luckily a school of kindly fish came to her rescue and nibbled through the stalk of the water lily, allowing her to float away. She soon made friends with a butterfly, who took one end of the sash of her dress while she held the other. The butterfly towed the lily pad along as if it were a small boat until it grew tired and had to fly away.

Feeling quite alone, Thumbelina was startled by a large beetle, who snatched her from her lily pad and took her off to a tree where he lived with many other beetles. They all decided that Thumbelina was ugly because she didn't look anything like a beetle. They soon sent her away.

Thumbelina lived alone in the forest during the summer and fall. As winter came on and the weather grew chillier, Thumbelina accepted the invitation of an elderly field mouse who offered her shelter if Thumbelina would keep house for her and tell her stories.

During the winter an old mole frequently came to visit the field mouse. It wasn't long before the old mole decided he wanted to marry Thumbelina. The mole was polite but gruesome, and Thumbelina fretted about the situation, fearing that one day she would have to give in and marry him.

One day the mole took Thumbelina and the field mouse into the underground tunnel where he lived and showed them a dead swallow he'd found there. When Thumbelina saw the bird, she was overwhelmed with compassion. She made a blanket of hay for the swallow and found her way back into the tunnel at night to wrap the bird in it. As she did so, she heard the bird's heart beating and realized the swallow wasn't dead, after all. She took care of it for the rest of the winter, and when spring came, the swallow tried to persuade Thumbelina to fly into the forest with him. But Thumbelina felt obliged to stay with the field mouse who had been kind enough to give her a place to live in the winter.

Even though it was spring, Thumbelina wasn't permitted to go outside in the sun. The old mole wanted her to tell him stories endlessly, and plans went ahead for him to marry Thumbelina. On the appointed wedding day Thumbelina sneaked off into the sunlight just long enough to say good-bye to the animals and flowers who had been her friends. Just as she was preparing to go back underground forever, she heard a fluttering of wings over her head. It was the swallow telling her she didn't have to marry the old mole. If she would just hop on his back, he would take her to the warm, sunny place where he was going.

Thumbelina agreed this time. Over hill and dale they flew, until finally the swallow set her gently on one of the petals of a beautiful flower. Thumbelina was just beginning to remember what it was like to live in a flower when she realized that someone else lived in this one. It was a tiny young man, not much bigger than herself, with a golden crown and wings. He explained that he was the king of all the flower spirits and asked her if she would like to be queen. Thumbelina felt as if all her dreams were coming true.

The spirits of the flowers came to welcome Thumbelina and to celebrate this great occasion. They all brought presents, but the best gift was a pair of gossamer wings so she could fly about her new kingdom with her handsome husband.

When the celebrations were over, the swallow said good-bye and flew north where he made a nest outside the window of a story-teller, to whom he sang of Thumbelina and her adventures.

THE ELVES AND THE SHOEMAKER

A hardworking and honest shoemaker found that in spite of his best efforts, he could not earn enough to live on. The day finally came when all he had in the world was a piece of leather just big enough to make one pair of shoes. In the evening he conscientiously cut out the leather, planning to make the shoes in the morning. Trusting his cares to God, the shoemaker went to bed.

The next day when he returned to his worktable, the shoemaker was astonished to see that the leather shoes were already made. He examined them carefully and found them perfectly made. He sold them that day for a good price and bought enough leather to make two more pairs. He cut the shoes out in the evening and went to bed early.

Once again the work was done in the morning. The shoemaker sold the shoes and bought more and more leather to make more and more shoes. This went on for some time.

At Christmastime he suggested to his wife that they stay up to see who was doing so much of his work. That night, at midnight, they watched as a pair of little elves stitched and hammered to make the shoes. The next day the wife suggested to the shoemaker that out of gratitude to the elves she should make them some nice clothes. The shoemaker agreed that this was a good idea, so his wife made a nice little outfit for each of them.

The elves came at midnight and were about to go to work when they saw the little outfits. Giddy with delight, they dressed themselves, then danced about as if they were at a party. Eventually they danced right out the door and into the night.

The elves did not come again, but the shoemaker and his wife lived happily for many years without any serious worries or problems.

RAPUNZEL

man and his wife yearned for a child of their own. At last it seemed they were to have one, and they waited patiently for it to come.

Though their house was modest, it stood next to a magical garden surrounded by a stone wall. From one of their windows the wife could just see over the wall to where the beautiful flowers and delicious vegetables grew. As the time grew near for her child to come, the woman found herself longing desperately for a salad green called rampion, which she knew was growing in the magical garden. She wanted it so much that she grew thin and frail and could eat no other food. Her husband became very worried about her and vowed that he would fetch her some of the rampion, though he privately feared being caught by the witch, Mother Gothel, who owned the magical garden. The first time he ventured into the garden, he was lucky and got away with an armful of rampion, which pleased his wife enormously. The second time he tried it, the witch caught him and called him a thief. She said he would have to be punished.

"Oh, please, Mother Gothel. I am not really a thief," he said, and explained that he and his wife were expecting a child and that her craving for the rampion was so great that he was afraid she would die if he didn't get it for her.

When the witch heard of the unborn baby, her attitude changed. "You can take as much of the rampion as you want for your wife," she said, "but you have to promise me one thing. When the child is born, if it is a girl, you must let me take her."

In blind fear of the witch's rage the husband agreed.

On the day the long-awaited baby was born, the witch appeared.

In spite of the parents' protests, she seized the child, saying she would name her Rapunzel, which was another word for *rampion* in that country.

Rapunzel grew to be very beautiful, and when she was twelve years old, she had long blond hair that glistened like spun gold. The witch took her off into the forest where a tower stood, surrounded by thornbushes. At the top was a tiny room with just one window. The witch locked Rapunzel in there and did away with the stairs that led to it. Rapunzel saw no one from her room in the tower except the witch, who came to visit her every few days. When the witch wished to see Rapunzel, she would stand at the bottom of the tower and call:

> *"Rapunzel, Rapunzel*
> *Let down your golden hair."*

Then Rapunzel would loosen her thick braids, twist them around the window latch, and let them drop to the witch below. Mother Gothel would then use them as a ladder to climb up to Rapunzel.

Several years went by. Then one day a young prince was riding through the woods and heard someone singing a slightly mournful sound. He followed the voice and realized it was coming from the tower. He returned to the tower the following day to listen again, and from his hiding place behind some bushes he watched Mother Gothel call out to Rapunzel to let down her golden hair.

The next afternoon the prince stood at the bottom of the tower and called out:

> *"Rapunzel, Rapunzel*
> *Let down your golden hair."*

The braids came tumbling down, and the prince climbed up as the witch had done. Rapunzel was frightened at first, but the prince was so gentle and kind that she knew she had nothing to fear. In fact, over time, she came to love him, and they married secretly in the desolate tower.

The prince returned often to visit Rapunzel, each time bringing a skein of silk that Rapunzel set about weaving into a ladder that she planned to use to flee the tower.

One day, when the ladder was nearly finished, Mother Gothel was coming to visit Rapunzel. The girl grew impatient waiting for her to climb up and said impetuously, "Mother Gothel, why does it take you so much longer than the king's son to come up?"

The witch knew right away what had happened and was furious. She whipped out a pair of scissors from her pocket and cut Rapunzel's braids off. Then, using the silken ladder to get out of the tower, she took Rapunzel deep into the woods and left her there all alone.

When the prince came to the tower that night to visit Rapunzel, he called to his bride to let down her hair. He climbed up as usual, only to meet Mother Gothel holding the braids. She ranted and raved at him and told him he would never see Rapunzel again. In terror the prince leapt from the tower to escape the witch. His fall was cushioned by the bushes upon which he fell, but his eyes were blinded by the thorns.

For a long time the prince wandered miserably in the forest. One day he happened to hear the crystalline voice that was so familiar to him. It was Rapunzel singing to the twin babies she had borne since leaving the tower. The prince found his way to Rapunzel, who recognized him instantly. Her tears of joy upon seeing him cleared his eyes instantly. Each carrying one twin boy, they made their way out of the forest to the prince's kingdom where they lived together happily for many years.

Better Read Aloud

Reading aloud is a pleasurable, important child-rearing experience, and much has been written about it. If you have not read Jim Trelease's book, *The Read-Aloud Handbook,* (Penguin, 1985), I encourage you to do so. Thoughtful parents will find it illuminating and inspiring.

The art of reading aloud borrows from the art of storytelling, the most obvious difference being the presence of a book. Trelease and other read-aloud proponents emphasize the value of hearing a story, especially as it encourages a child to read. When you read aloud to younger children, you can let your child handle the book and see the pictures. Young children, especially toddlers, will not be able to follow a story directly, so you can stop almost anywhere to discuss what you are reading without doing harm. With older children,

of course, you will be trying to approximate the storytelling experience, so stopping and starting could mar your presentation. Relax and let your voice communicate that which you are reading in an easy, rolling rhythm.

On pages 67–69 we have presented twenty-seven of our favorite read-aloud or "lap" books, those works which we feel are better read than told. They are characterized by unforgettable illustrations, quirky characters, and plot lines that range from the subtle to the outlandish. These books are not part of the oral tradition but are modern-day classics, and your home library should include many of them. Our list is utterly opinionated, occasionally sentimental, and born of our memories, informal polls with teachers and friends, and the spirited guidance of the New York Public Library.

TOM THUMB

A peasant and his wife were bemoaning the fact that they had no children. "If we had just one," the wife sighed, "even if it was just as big as my thumb, I would be perfectly happy."

Not long afterward, a little boy was born to the woman and her husband. He was perfectly healthy but only as big as a thumb. Because he was so tiny, the couple named him Tom Thumb. Though the child was lively and bright, he never grew so much as an inch.

Years later when his father was going into the forest to cut wood, Tom offered to bring the cart to hold the wood. He asked his mother to harness the horse. The horse then pulled the cart as Tom sat in his ear, directing him where to go. Two travelers in the woods noticed the driverless cart at the same time they heard Tom shouting to the horse. When the cart arrived at the place where Tom's father was working, Tom jumped down out of the horse's ear. The travelers saw all this and decided they could make a bundle of money exhibiting Tom in a circus. They made Tom's father an offer to buy him, which Tom persuaded his father to accept, promising he would soon be back.

Tom went along for a while with the two men, seated on the brim of one of their hats. Then he jumped down, thanked them for the ride, and scampered into a mouse hole. After looking everywhere for him, the two men were obliged to go on without Tom. Venturing out to look for a more pleasant place to sleep, Tom found an empty snail shell and crawled inside. From there he overheard two thieves plotting to rob the rich parson. Tom offered to help by sneaking between the iron bars into the parson's room and handing out all the gold and silver he could find. The thieves thought this was a fine idea, until Tom foiled their plans by speaking so loudly to them that the cook and the maid woke up and frightened the thieves away. Tom slipped out into the barn and slept so soundly for the rest of the night that he was gobbled up by the cow for breakfast. Inside the cow's mouth, he negotiated his way carefully between the cow's teeth and into his belly. Then he called out as loudly as he could, "Please don't feed me. Don't feed me."

The maid who was milking the cow was scared out of her wits and went to get the pastor to hear the talking cow. When he heard Tom's voice in the cow, he was convinced the animal was bewitched and gave orders for it to be slaughtered. Tom survived that ordeal because he was in the cow's stomach, which was flung in one piece into a pile of manure. As Tom was figuring how to get out of his predicament, a wolf came by and swallowed the stomach in one gulp. Knowing that the wolf was probably still hungry, Tom called to the wolf from his stomach. "I know where you can get a really good meal," he said.

Tom described the way to his own house, spurring the wolf on with details about the goodies he would find there. When they arrived, the house was quiet and the wolf was able to sneak through the grating that protected the house. There he found all the food he'd been promised and ate his fill. When he was ready to leave, he discovered he'd grown so fat, he couldn't fit through the grating. Tom shouted and screamed until he had awakened his parents. They were ready to tear the wolf apart until they realized his voice was coming from inside the wolf's body. They knocked the wolf on the head and carefully removed their little boy from the wolf's stomach. The reunion was joyfully celebrated.

SNOW WHITE AND THE SEVEN DWARFS

lovely queen pricked her finger with a needle while she was sewing by the window. Three drops of blood fell on the snowy white linen in her lap. She thought to herself, "I wish I had a daughter with lips as red as blood, skin as white as this linen and hair as black as the ebony window frame."

Before long, the queen's wish was granted, and a beautiful baby girl was born to her. She named the child Snow White. Soon after the baby was born, the lovely queen died, and the king married again. The new queen was beautiful, but vain and cruel, and didn't want anyone to be more beautiful than she. Each day the queen looked into her magic mirror and said,

"Mirror, mirror on the wall,
Who's the fairest one of all?"

Usually the mirror replied,

"You are the fairest one of all."

But one day the mirror answered that Snow White was fairer than she. Furious, the queen instructed one of her hunters to take Snow White into the forest and kill her. She asked that Snow White's heart be brought back to her in a jeweled box to prove that the deed was done.

The hunter could not bear to harm Snow White, so he told her to run off into the woods and never come near the castle again. On his way back to the castle the hunter killed a young boar and put its heart in a jeweled box. He gave this to the queen and she was delighted, thinking now that Snow White was dead.

Alone and afraid in the forest, Snow White searched for a safe place to sleep. She caught sight of a cottage that looked so inviting, and she went up to it and found the door unlocked. Inside she found that there were seven of almost everything: a little table was set with seven knives and forks, seven bowls, seven mugs, and upstairs were seven small beds, side by side. Snow White toppled onto the nearest bed, intending to sleep for just a few minutes.

While Snow White slept, seven little men strutted through the woods, on their way home. As soon as they entered the cottage, they sensed that someone else was there. When they looked upstairs, they found Snow White, sound asleep. The next morning she told them about her wicked stepmother and asked if she could stay with them. They said she would be welcome but warned her never to open the door to strangers, lest the wicked queen discover that she was there.

By this time the queen had consulted her magic mirror, hoping to hear that she was the fairest in the land. But the mirror answered,

"In the woods where seven dwarfs dwell,
Snow White lives, both fair and well."

Realizing that the hunter had tricked her, the queen decided to do away with Snow White herself. Dressed like a peddler, she set out into the woods with a bundle of combs and laces. One of the combs was poisoned, and that she intended to offer to Snow White. As she drew near the cottage she called out, "Combs and laces for sale." Snow White remembered what the dwarfs had said about opening the door, but the queen persuaded her to crack it just enough to pass the comb through. Snow White couldn't resist combing her hair with it. As soon as she did, the poison began to work and she fell to the floor.

The seven dwarfs arrived home just in time to rescue Snow White from the full effect of the poison.

At the castle the queen consulted her magic mirror to hear again the bad news that Snow White lived. Livid, she disguised herself as an ugly old woman. She planned to put Snow White to sleep forever with an apple that was both yellow and red and soaked on the red side with poison. She hobbled off toward the cottage calling out, "Bright, juicy apples for sale." She tempted Snow White with the apple through the open window. To show her that it was perfectly good to eat, she bit into the yellow half herself and gave the poisoned half to Snow White, who bit it and fell to the floor, apparently dead. The wicked queen hastened back to the castle where her magic mirror told her that "she was the fairest one of all."

When the seven dwarfs found Snow White that evening, they could not revive her. They mourned her for several days and nights, then placed her body in a glass coffin with her name in gold on the outside. They put the coffin in a special place near the cottage.

One day a prince riding through the woods saw Snow White in her glass coffin. He thought she was so beautiful that he asked the dwarfs' permission to take her in her coffin to his palace where he could gaze at her forever. As the prince's men carried the coffin through the woods, one of them stumbled, causing the piece of poisoned apple to fall out of Snow White's mouth. She awoke from her deep sleep and was told by the prince that she was safe with him. "I want you to be my wife," he said, and she agreed.

A gala wedding was held. As the queen was dressing for it she checked her magic mirror and was told that the bride was the fairest woman in the land. Incredulous, the queen rushed to see for herself. When she saw Snow White, she collapsed and died. Snow White and the prince lived happily together for many years to come.

ANNOTATION

Other versions of "Snow White and the Seven Dwarfs," particularly Walt Disney's, emphasize Snow White's close relationship with all the animals in the woods, who endeavor to protect her from the first moment she is alone in the forest. The image of them pecking and clawing at the wicked queen as she tries to give Snow White the poisoned apple is particularly powerful.

In Disney's version of the tale we are told that the wicked queen casts a spell of endless sleep upon Snow White from which she can only be awakened by a lover's kiss. She feels quite certain that no lover would ever find Snow White asleep in the woods. It is the prince's kiss that restores life to Snow White, who promptly agrees to marry him. After bidding the dwarfs good-bye, she rides off with the prince to his Castle of Dreams Come True.

BOOKS TO READ ALOUD TOGETHER

Bemelmans, Ludwig. *Madeline.* Viking, 1939. In this enchanting book little Madeline and her companions in the French orphanage are first introduced. There are several equally charming books in the series about Madeline.

Burton, Virginia L. *Mike Mulligan and His Steam Shovel.* Houghton-Mifflin, 1939. Mike Mulligan races against time to dig a cellar with his steam shovel in one day.

Carle, Eric. *The Very Hungry Caterpillar.* Collins, 1970. The very young reader learns the names of all the things a caterpillar eats on his way to becoming a butterfly.

de Brunhoff, Jean. *The Story of Babar the Little Elephant.* Random House, 1960. Orphaned Babar becomes king of the elephants. Other books in the series follow him from one adventure to another.

DuVoisin, Roger. *Petunia.* Knopf, 1950. Petunia the goose thinks the grass is greener in her neighbors' yard, but she eventually decides there's no place like home. There are more books about Petunia by the same author.

Ets, Marie Hall. *Gilberto and the Wind.* Knopf, 1950. A little Mexican boy makes friends with the unpredictable wind.

————. *Play With Me.* Viking, 1955. A little girl discovers that if she sits very still, the animals and insects she wants to play with will come to her.

Flack, Marjorie. *Angus and the Cat.* Doubleday, 1930. Angus is a Scottie dog who becomes upset when a new cat invades his territory.

Gag, Wanda. *Millions of Cats.* Coward, 1928. In this modern classic an old man searches for the perfect cat for his wife. He finds thousands, millions, of them and can't choose just one, so he brings them all home.

Johnson, Crockett. *Harold and the Purple Crayon.* Harper and Row, 1955. A small boy has a fantasy of going for a walk late at night. With his purple crayon he draws all he thinks he hopes to find along the way.

Keats, Ezra Jack. *John Henry: An American Legend.* Pantheon, 1965. Bold illustrations help tell the story of the hero who was born with a hammer in his hand.

———. *The Snowy Day.* Viking, 1962. A young black boy discovers the excitement of playing in the snow.

Kellogg, Steven. *Pinkerton, Behave!* Dial, 1979. Any child with a puppy in the house will be amused by Pinkerton, who can't seem to behave. When told to come, he jumps out the window. Asked to fetch, he chews up the newspaper. But he becomes a hero in the end.

Leaf, Munro. *The Story of Ferdinand.* Illustrated by Robert Lawson. Viking, 1936. Young Ferdinand the bull feels no need to be fierce in bullfights. He prefers to live quietly, passing his time smelling flowers.

Marshall, James. *George and Martha.* Houghton-Mifflin, 1972. George and Martha are two hippos who learn the true meaning of friendship. There are more George and Martha stories for those who are amused by this one.

McCloskey, Roberta. *Make Way for Ducklings.* Viking, 1941. We follow Mrs. Mallard and her eight ducklings on their treacherous journey to their new home on an island in the Boston Public Garden.

Milne, A. A. *Pooh's Pot o' Honey.* E. P. Dutton, 1968. This is a collection of four favorite Pooh stories in tiny individual volumes packaged in one boxed set.

Minarik, Else Holmelund. *A Kiss for Little Bear.* Illustrated by Maurice Sendak. Grandma Bear's kiss takes a long time to reach Little Bear as it is passed along whisper-down-the-lane style from one animal to another.

Parrish, Peggy. *Amelia Bedelia.* Illustrated by Fritz Seibel. Harper and Row, 1963. Amelia creates disaster as she does *exactly* what she's told: she "dresses the turkey" in shorts, "dusts the furniture" with dusting powder, and "puts the lights out" on the clothesline. For those who love her, there are several sequels by Parrish about Amelia.

Potter, Beatrix. *The Tale of Peter Rabbit.* Frederick Warne and Co., 1902; Dover, 1972. In this book readers meet naughty Peter Rabbit and his friends. Their adventures are continued in several other engaging animal tales by Potter.

Rey, Hans A. *Curious George.* Houghton-Mifflin, 1941. Amusing illustrations enhance the story of an inquisitive monkey who gets into trouble living in the city before he takes up residence in a zoo.

Sendak, Maurice. *Where the Wild Things Are.* Harper and Row, 1963. This modern classic is about a boy sent to his room for cavorting around in his wolf costume. He falls asleep and dreams of going where the wild things are, to rule them and share their antics, until he is overcome by longing to be where "someone loves him best."

Slobodkina, Esphyr. *Caps for Sale.* William R. Scott, 1940. A peddler carries the caps he sells in a stack on top of his head. When he sits down under a tree to rest, some mischievous monkeys steal them, but the clever peddler gets them back.

Steig, William. *The Amazing Bone.* Farrar, Straus and Giroux, 1976. In this suspenseful tale of a heroine pig, the day is saved by the power of a magical bone.

Seuss, Dr. *And to Think That I Saw It On Mulberry Street.* Hale, 1937. A small boy tells a tall tale about what he saw on Mulberry Street when all he saw was a horse and wagon.

————. *Dr. Horton Hatches the Egg.* Random House, 1940. Dr. Horton fills in for a Lazy Mazie bird hatching her egg. What emerges from the egg is not what anyone expected.

Zion, Gene. *Harry the Dirty Dog.* Illustrated by Margaret B. Graham. Harper and Row, 1956. Children love Harry, who gets so dirty that no one in his entire family can recognize him. The artwork and simple, expressive text make this book a perfect choice for very young children.

CHAPTER TWO

Rhymes

"Not marble, nor the gilded monuments
Of princes, shall outlive this powerful rime."
—William Shakespeare, *Sonnet 55*

INTRODUCTION

My husband has a theory that in the grand order of things we live twice: once as ourselves alone, and the second time through our children. This theory usually receives eloquent expression when I discover him "checking out" our daughter's sled on a winter's afternoon, or "fixing" her battery-operated deep-sea diver in the swimming pool.

If indeed we get to live this wondrous thing called life two times, then my second time around started with nursery rhymes. Once I started sharing them with my daughters, I became strangely childlike and embarrassingly addicted. It is difficult to describe, and I do so at risk of sounding a fool, but I find that half delirious, utterly blank state of chanting nursery rhymes completely seductive. Nursery rhymes are meditations for children. I like them.

If you don't believe me, try one right now. Try one you know, like "Jack Sprat." Lift your voice to that half chanting, half crying-out pitch you employed as a child. Your head is bobbing a bit, isn't it? Now say it over and over again to the beat in your own mind. Aren't you tempted to say it louder and faster? Isn't this good fun?

Now you can see why children have chanted nursery rhymes for hundreds of years, and why Mother Goose will always be a feature of childhood. These rhymes have enduring, almost primal qualities of strong rhythm, nonsensical words, and brevity. As a parent, you will want to introduce your new child to these rhymes immediately. Infants respond to the happy cadence of nursery rhymes. Toddlers learn language from your repetition and enunciation. Preschoolers learn syntax and develop memory skills by chanting on their own. At five years old, your child has a vocabulary of two thousand words, and nursery rhymes are crucial to the development of your child's speech and comprehension.

Nursery rhymes predate all educational theories, of course. Some of them are political satire, others are just silly poems that worked their way into the oral tradition. Mother Goose, herself, is rather a mystery. We do not know if she was a goose or a mother, or if she existed at all. (See page 81.) But under her heading comes some of the best childhood verse ever written.

Now, to get the most out of nursery rhymes, I suggest reviewing the rhymes that follow and picking out one every week or so to memorize. This shouldn't be difficult. Most of them are short and already on the tip of your tongue. As for the longer ones, it is good discipline for you. Memorizing verse will build your memory skills and will help in your ability to tell stories.

Once you have learned the words, you will want to create inventive ways to use them. All nursery rhymes can be chanted just for fun, of course, but since we are always seeking ways to rid ourselves of two birds with one stone, I suggest you study these rhymes for more than mere linguistic frolic. For instance, "One, Two" is a superb rhyme for teaching your child how to count, as well as what a shoe, door, stick, gate, and so on, are. "A Diller, A Dollar" is a fun way to teach your child about time. "Jack, Be Nimble" can teach your child to jump. I could go on and on. You can see that with a little imagination these rhymes can enliven the most rudimentary lesson in life.

When you recite a rhyme, you also have an opportunity to help your child's diction. Speak very clearly. Allow your child to see your mouth. Exaggerate a little bit. Enunciate all of your words, and emphasize the rhyming words. You will give your child a close-up lesson in speech without preaching to him or putting him on the line.

The point is that nursery rhymes are rich and varied verses. Let your child benefit fully from these rhymes; allow the bright and charmingly antiquated language to sink in; let the rhythm move your child mentally and physically; be sure the content, however foolish, is not lost on him.

Nursery rhymes are good literature. They add wit and bounce to your child's life, and if they cause you to be a child again, all the better.

HOT-CROSS BUNS

Hot-cross Buns!
Hot-cross Buns!
  One a penny, two a penny,
Hot-cross Buns!
Hot-cross Buns!
Hot-cross Buns!
  If ye have no daughters,
Give them to your sons.

LITTLE TOMMY TUCKER

Little Tommy Tucker
Sings for his supper;
What shall he eat?
White bread and butter.
How shall he cut it,
Without e'er a knife?
How will he be married
Without e'er a wife?

A DILLER, A DOLLAR

A diller, a dollar,
A ten o'clock scholar,
What makes you come so soon?
You used to come at ten o'clock,
But now you come at noon.

LITTLE JACK HORNER

Little Jack Horner sat in a corner,
Eating a Christmas pie;
He put in his thumb and pulled out a plum,
And said, "What a good boy am I!"

TOM, TOM

Tom, Tom, the piper's son,
Stole a pig, and away he run!
The pig was eat, and Tom was beat,
And Tom went roaring down the street.

Rhyme and Reading

Over the past few decades we have learned that there is a method to Mother Goose's sometimes apparent madness that is born of the extraordinary value rhyming has to the acquisition of reading skills.

Rhymes are a key to the first confrontations with language. As your child hears them and repeats them to himself, he is learning about the differences and similarities in sound. Most children experiment with rhymes on their own, like *yuck, tuck, shuck,* or *bold, dold, pold.* They seize the chance to play with words they've just learned and they try their hand at inventing new, and often comical, ones.

Long before your child enters kindergarten, he is familiar with certain patterns in words, so when the teacher asks him to collect a group of words with *an* in all of them, he is ready to respond with *can, man, tan,* and others. That is his first important step toward reading. With the help of the teacher he learns how different consonants and consonant combinations can be written in front of core sounds like *an,* to make *fan, span,* and *than.* As you encourage your child to play with rhymes you foster a critical sense of sounds, which ultimately will lead him to the phonetic acquisition of the language.

SOLOMON GRUNDY

Solomon Grundy,
Born on Monday,
Christened on Tuesday,
Married on Wednesday,
Took ill on Thursday,
Worse on Friday,
Died on Saturday,
Buried on Sunday:
This is the end
Of Solomon Grundy.

ONE, TWO

One, two,
Buckle my shoe;
Three, four,
Shut the door;
Five, six,
Pick up sticks;
Seven, eight,
Lay them straight;
Nine, ten,
A good fat hen;
Eleven, twelve,
Who will delve?
Thirteen, fourteen,
Maids a-courting;
Fifteen, sixteen,
Maids a-kissing;
Seventeen, eighteen,
Maids a-waiting;
Nineteen, twenty,
My stomach's empty.

THE HOUSE THAT JACK BUILT

This is the house that Jack built.

This is the malt
That lay in the house that Jack built.

This is the rat,
That ate the malt,
That lay in the house that Jack built.

This is the cat,
That killed the rat,
That ate the malt,
That lay in the house that Jack built.

This is the dog,
That worried the cat,
That killed the rat,
That ate the malt,
That lay in the house that Jack built.

This is the cow with the crumpled horn,
That tossed the dog,
That worried the cat,
That killed the rat,
That ate the malt,
That lay in the house that Jack built.

This is the maiden all forlorn,
That milked the cow with the crumpled horn,
That tossed the dog,
That worried the cat,
That killed the rat,
That ate the malt,
That lay in the house that Jack built.

This is the man all tattered and torn,
That kissed the maiden all forlorn,
That milked the cow with the crumpled horn,
That tossed the dog,
That worried the cat,
That killed the rat,
That ate the malt,
That lay in the house that Jack built.

This is the priest all shaven and shorn
That married the man all tattered and torn,
That kissed the maiden all forlorn,
That milked the cow with the crumpled horn,
That tossed the dog,
That worried the cat,
That killed the rat,
That ate the malt,
That lay in the house that Jack built.

This is the cock that crowed in the morn,
That waked the priest all shaven and shorn,
That married the man all tattered and torn,
That kissed the maiden all forlorn,
That milked the cow with the crumpled horn,
That tossed the dog,
That worried the cat,
That killed the rat,
That ate the malt,
That lay in the house that Jack built.

This is the farmer sowing his corn,
That kept the cock that crowed in the morn,
That waked the priest all shaven and shorn,
That married the man all tattered and torn,
That kissed the maiden all forlorn,
That milked the cow with the crumpled horn,
That tossed the dog,
That worried the cat,
That killed the rat,
That ate the malt,
That lay in the house that Jack built.

QUEEN OF HEARTS

The Queen of Hearts,
  She made some tarts,
  All on a summer's day;
The Knave of Hearts,
He stole those tarts,
  And took them clean away.

The King of Hearts
Called for the tarts,
  And beat the Knave full sore;
The Knave of Hearts
Brought back the tarts,
  And vowed he'd steal no more.

IF WISHES WERE HORSES

If wishes were horses,
  Beggars would ride;
If turnips were watches,
  I would wear one by my side.

JACK, BE NIMBLE

Jack, be nimble,
  Jack, be quick;
Jack, jump over
  The candlestick.

Who Is Mother Goose?

One of the great mysteries of children's literature is the where-abouts and, I suppose, the who-abouts, of Mother Goose. It seems that over the centuries almost every culture has made a claim on her, and the sometimes nonsensical explanations of her person run con-sistent with the nature of her work—that is, if she is a "her" at all.

The Americans have their version. For us, Mother Goose was Mistress Elizabeth Goose, who lived in Boston in the early eigh-teenth century. She had a flock of grandchildren, it seems, and used to share with them the verses she learned at her own mother's knee. Her husband, Thomas Fleet, happened to be a printer and decided to print the verses, it is suggested, out of malice. Apparently he had heard them recited once too often. In any case, a collection of them was printed in 1719 and entitled *Songs for the Nursery, or Mother Goose's Melodies.*

Much as one would love to believe the American claim, there is a case against Mistress Goose of Boston. In seventeenth-century France, a book on storytelling was published by a gentleman called Loret; his book was tagged *Comme un conte de ma mère l'Oye*—like a Mother Goose story. And in 1697, the storyteller Charles Perrault published, under his ten-year-old son's name, a collection of stories called *Histoires ou contes du temps passé.*

But, in truth, Mother Goose might be even older. The Baring-Gould's *Annotated Mother Goose* suggests that she might be Bertha, the wife of Pepin and mother of Charlemagne, who was known to her subjects by a name derived from the size and shape of her foot. We don't know which, but it was either a clubfoot or gout that caused the condition, and she came to be called Queen Goose Foot or Goose-footed Bertha. We also know that this poor woman spent most of her days spinning while hordes of children gathered around her, listening to her stories. Thus the French came to describe any tall tale as one told at the "time when Queen Bertha spun."

RIDE A COCKHORSE

Ride a cockhorse to Banbury Cross,
To see an old lady upon a white horse;
Rings on her fingers and bells on her toes,
And so she makes music wherever she goes.

HIGGLEY PIGGLEY

Higgley Piggley,
My black hen,
She lays eggs
For gentlemen;
Sometimes nine,
And sometimes ten.
Higgley Piggley,
My black hen!

WEE WILLIE WINKIE

Wee Willie Winkie runs through the town,
Upstairs and downstairs in his nightgown,
Rapping at the window, crying through the lock,
"Are the children in their beds, for now it's
eight o'clock?"

OLD MOTHER HUBBARD

Old Mother Hubbard
Went to the cupboard
  To get her poor dog a bone;
But when she came there
The cupboard was bare,
  And so the poor dog had none.

She went to the baker's
  To buy him some bread,
But when she came back
  The poor dog was dead.

She went to the joiner's
  To buy him a coffin,
But when she came back
  The poor dog was laughing.

She took a clean dish
  To get him some tripe,
But when she came back
  He was smoking his pipe.

She went to the fishmonger's
  To buy him some fish,
And when she came back
  He was licking the dish.

She went to the alehouse
  To get him some beer,
But when she came back
  The dog sat in a chair.

She went to the tavern
  For white wine and red,
But when she came back
  The dog stood on his head.

She went to the hatter's
  To buy him a hat,
But when she came back
  He was feeding the cat.

She went to the barber's
  To buy him a wig,
But when she came back
  He was dancing a jig.

She went to the fruiterer's
  To buy him some fruit,
But when she came back
  He was playing the flute.

She went to the tailor's
  To buy him a coat,
But when she came back
  He was riding a goat.

She went to the cobbler's
  To buy him some shoes,
But when she came back
  He was reading the news.

She went to the seamstress
  To buy him some linen,
But when she came back
  The dog was spinning.

She went to the hosier's
  To buy him some hose,
But when she came back
  He was dressed in his clothes

The dame made a curtsy,
  The dog made a bow;
The dame said, "Your servant,"
  The dog said, "Bow, wow."

DEEDLE DEEDLE DUMPLING

Deedle deedle dumpling, my son John
Went to bed with his trousers on;
One shoe off, the other shoe on,
Deedle deedle dumpling, my son John.

Bringing Rhyme Into Everyday Life

By the time your child is three months old, he is ready to respond to rhythm and rhyme. You'll notice him cooing and beginning to make vowellike sounds. He'll delight in your imitating his sounds, so do so, and then add variations. For example, if he says, "Ma-ma-ma-ma-moo," you repeat it, and then see if he will imitate you saying "La-la-la-la-loo." Try singing some of his phrases and yours. He'll be amused, even if he is not quite sure what you are doing.

The best time to share rhymes is when you get tired of baby talk, something with which I had a truly hard time. I suppose it was my Scandinavian blood, but something made goo-gooing just impossible for me. I took refuge in the nursery rhymes and would recite them when I was cooking or changing my daughter or dressing her. Once you have a ready arsenal of these rhymes memorized and ready to go, you can use them throughout the day.

The important thing is that you infuse these rhymes into daily rituals. "Three Men in a Tub" at bathtime. "Old Mother Hubbard" in the kitchen. "One, Two" for an afternoon game. Don't wait for a special time of the day or think you must have "rhyming sessions." Scatter these rhymes throughout your day, at home and away, but always at the moment you have made for them.

THREE LITTLE KITTENS

Three little kittens lost their mittens,
And they began to cry,
"O mother dear,
We very much fear
That we have lost our mittens."

"Lost your mittens!
You naughty kittens!
Then you shall have no pie."
"Mee-ow, mee-ow, mee-ow."
"No, you shall have no pie."
"Mee-ow, mee-ow, mee-ow."

The three little kittens found their mittens,
And they began to cry,
"O mother dear,
See here, see here,
See, we have found our mittens!"

"Put on your mittens,
You silly kittens,
And you may have some pie."
"Purr-r, purr-r, purr-r,
Oh, let us have the pie.
Purr-r, purr-r, purr-r."

The three little kittens put on their mittens,
And soon ate up the pie;
"O mother dear,
We greatly fear
That we have soiled our mittens."

"Soiled your mittens!
You naughty kittens!"
Then they began to sigh,
"Mee-ow, mee-ow, mee-ow."

The three little kittens washed their mittens,
And hung them out to dry;
"O mother dear,
Do you not hear,
That we have washed our mittens?"

"Washed your mittens!
Oh, you're good kittens.
But I smell a rat close by!"
"Hush, hush! Mee-ow, mee-ow!
We smell a rat close by!
Mee-ow, mee-ow, mee-ow!"

TO MARKET, TO MARKET

To market, to market, to buy a fat pig;
Home again, home again, jiggety-jig.
To market, to market, to buy a fat hog;
Home again, home again, jiggety-jog.

WHAT ARE LITTLE BOYS MADE OF?

What are little boys made of, made of;
What are little boys made of?
"Snaps and snails, and puppy dogs' tails;
And that's what little boys are made of, made of."

What are little girls made of, made of;
What are little girls made of?
"Sugar and spice, and all that's nice;
And that's what little girls are made of, made of."

THERE WAS AN OLD WOMAN

There was an old woman who lived in a shoe;
She had so many children she didn't know what
  to do;
She gave them some broth without any bread;
She whipped them all soundly and put them to bed.

PEASE PORRIDGE HOT

Pease porridge hot,
  Pease porridge cold,
Pease porridge in the pot,
  Nine days old.
Some like it hot,
  Some like it cold,
Some like it in the pot,
  Nine days old.

LUCY LOCKET

Lucy Locket lost her pocket,
  Kitty Fisher found it;
Nothing in it, nothing in it,
  But the binding round it.

LITTLE BO-PEEP

Little Bo-Peep has lost her sheep,
And can't tell where to find them;
Leave them alone, and they'll come home,
Wagging their tails behind them.

Little Bo-Peep fell fast asleep,
And dreamt she heard them bleating;
When she awoke, 'twas a joke—
Ah! cruel vision so fleeting.

Then up she took her little crook,
Determined for to find them;
What was her joy to behold them nigh,
Wagging their tails behind them.

THERE WAS A CROOKED MAN

There was a crooked man, and he went a
  crooked mile,
He found a crooked sixpence against a crooked stile.
He bought a crooked cat, which caught a crooked
  mouse,
And they all lived together in a crooked little house.

Building Memory With Rhyme

Children love to hear rhymes over and over. Becoming familiar with them builds a sense of security about what is predictable in their everyday experience. Once your child hears a rhyme a couple of times, he will want to chant it along with you. Here are a couple of excellent ways you can help him in the process of memorization.

- You say the first line of a rhyme. When you come to the next rhyming word, let him fill it in. Alternate until you have finished the rhyme. Example: Peter, Peter, pumpkin eater, had a wife and couldn't ———. Put her in a pumpkin shell, and there he kept her very ———.

- Once your child has learned to rhyme using the technique just described, you can expand the game using lines instead of words. For instance, you say, "To market, to market, to buy a fat pig," and let your child fill in with the next line "Home again, home again, jiggety jig." As your child learns more and more rhymes, let him fill in with as many lines as he can. You can lend support by filling in a word or two, as required.

- When your child has a fair repertoire of rhymes he can recite easily, have him try a comprehension game with you. You, for example, can say a rhyme with an incorrect word. "Old King Cole was a merry old *bowl.*" Have your child correct you, and discuss why the word he said was right and why the one you used was wrong.

LADYBUG, LADYBUG

Ladybug, ladybug,
Fly away home,
Your house is on fire,
And your children will burn.

THREE MEN IN A TUB

Hey, rub-a-dub-dub, three men in a tub,
And who do you think were there?
The butcher, the baker, the candlestick-maker,
And all had come from the fair.

LITTLE BOY BLUE

Little boy blue, come blow your horn,
The sheep's in the meadow, the cow's in
* the corn.*
Where's the boy that looks after the
* sheep?*
He's under the haycock, fast asleep.
* Will you wake him? No, not I;*
* For if I do, he'll be sure to cry.*

PUSSYCAT, PUSSYCAT

Pussycat, pussycat,
* Where have you been?*
I've been to London
* To look at the Queen.*
Pussycat, pussycat,
* What did you there?*
I frightened a little mouse
* Under the chair.*

OLD KING COLE

Old King Cole
Was a merry old soul,
And a merry old soul was he;
He called for his pipe,
And he called for his bowl,
And he called for his fiddlers three.

Every fiddler, he had a fiddle,
And a very fine fiddle had he;
Twee Tweedle dee, tweedle dee,
* went the fiddler.*
Oh, there's none so rare,
As can compare
With King Cole and his fiddlers three!

HEY DIDDLE DIDDLE

Hey diddle diddle!
  The cat and the fiddle;
The cow jumped over the moon.
The little dog laughed
  To see such craft;
And the dish ran away with the spoon.

LITTLE MISS MUFFET

Little Miss Muffet sat on her tuffet,
  Eating of curds and whey;
Along came a spider and sat down beside her,
  And frightened Miss Muffet away.

MARY, MARY

Mary, Mary, quite contrary,
How does your garden grow?
With silver bells and cockle shells
And pretty maids all in a row.

PETER PIPER

Peter Piper picked a peck of
pickled peppers;
A peck of pickled peppers Peter Piper
picked;
If Peter Piper picked a peck of pickled
peppers,
Where's the peck of pickled peppers Peter
Piper picked?

PETER, PETER, PUMPKIN EATER

Peter, Peter, Pumpkin Eater,
Had a wife and couldn't keep her.
He put her in a pumpkin shell,
And there he kept her very well.

Peter, Peter, Pumpkin Eater,
Had another and didn't love her.
Peter learned to read and spell,
And then he loved her very well.

HICKORY DICKORY DOCK

Hickory dickory dock,
The mouse ran up the clock;
The clock struck one,
And down he run,
Hickory dickory dock.

JACK SPRAT

Jack Sprat could eat no fat,
  His wife could eat no lean;
And so, betwixt them both (you see)
  They licked the platter clean.

GEORGEY PORGEY

Georgey Porgey, pudding and pie,
Kissed the girls and made them cry;
When the boys come out to play
Georgey Porgey runs away.

SING A SONG OF SIXPENCE

Sing a song of sixpence,
  A pocket full of rye;
Four-and-twenty blackbirds
  Baked in a pie;
When the pie was opened
  The birds began to sing;
Wasn't that a dainty dish
  To set before the King?
The King was in his countinghouse,
  Counting out his money;
The Queen was in the parlor,
  Eating bread and honey;
The maid was in the garden
  Hanging out the clothes;
When up came a blackbird
  And snapt off her nose.

HUMPTY DUMPTY

Humpty Dumpty sat on a wall,
Humpty Dumpty had a great fall;
Not all the King's horses,
Nor all the King's men,
Could put Humpty Dumpty together again.

SIMPLE SIMON

Simple Simon met a pieman
Going to the fair;
Says Simple Simon to the pieman,
"Let me taste your ware."

Says the pieman to Simple Simon,
"Show me first your penny."
Says Simple Simon to the pieman,
"Indeed, I have not any."

Simple Simon went a-fishing,
For to catch a whale:
All the water he had got
Was in his mother's pail.

SEE-SAW, MARGERY DAW

See-saw, Margery Daw,
Jenny shall have a new master;
And she shall have but a penny a day,
Because she can't work any faster.

CHAPTER THREE
Fables

"Tut, tut, child," said the Duchess.
"Everything's got a moral, if only you can find it."
—Lewis Carroll, *Alice's Adventures in Wonderland*

INTRODUCTION

Fables are wonderful, sometimes haunting, stories that are created by people who have a very affectionate (and patient) view of themselves, their fellows, and our impossibly human, human nature.

Fables are different from fairy tales. Fairy tales are leisurely and romantic; fables are crisp and dispassionate. Fables almost always have a serious moral, but it is more a case of intelligent gossip over a fence than a sermon from a pulpit. Fables do not take themselves too seriously, and neither should we when we tell them.

All of us know at least a handful of fables, whether we know how to tell them or not. Tales like "The Hare and the Tortoise" and "The Boy Who Cried Wolf" are so often told that they have become phrases in the language. When we are sly, we are as sly as one of Aesop's foxes; when we are dull, we are like one of his slow oxen. Even if we are not familiar with all of his fables, we are unavoidably familiar with the characters in them.

Aesop is the father of fables, though, like Mother Goose, we are not quite sure he ever existed. It is commonly accepted that he was a Greek slave who used to entertain his master, and all who would listen, with his witty stories, some 2,700 years ago. About two hundred stories are credited to Aesop. His form, which almost exclusively used animals, has been used throughout history by everyone from Rudyard Kipling to George Orwell and James Thurber. Recently the fable has appeared most often in cartoons: Charles Schultz's *Peanuts,* Walt Kelly's old *Pogo,* and even *Road Runner* are a few examples that come to mind.

Fables give us "people lessons" in doses we can take, but they should never be prescribed to a young child who needs correction or punishment. Fables are not meant to instruct as much as they are intended to illuminate. Life teaches us the lessons; fables shed light on the lessons. If, for example, you told your child "The Fox and the Crow" just after he was duped by some "false flatterers," you could lead him to believe the world is choking with liars. On the other hand, if you told him the same tale in a neutral context, just because it is a wonderful story, he would take tremendous insights from it and subconsciously apply it to the children he has known or the experiences he has had.

Obviously fables won't mean much to a two-year-old. They are suited for children at least four or five years old, and even then the child must have had a fair amount of social interaction. To appreciate the human condition one has to know humans. Fables should be told well after you have been sharing fairy tales, and probably before you tell legends and myths. I have heard them told in strategy sessions on Madison Avenue and to fifth-graders by a spellbinding librarian. Once you are ready for fables, you cannot hear them too often.

The fables that follow are to be retold just as they are, without too much embellishment or tinkering. You can dabble with your own use of language, but do not lengthen them too much; they should retain their elegant simplicity. Fables are like proverbs: They can be told over and over again. If your child wants to discuss the moral of the story, well, okay, but it is not imperative. Like any tale, fables will say the most if they are unadorned, unexpected, and given from the heart.

THE FARMER
AND HIS SONS

 wealthy farmer who wasn't well and felt that his days were numbered called his sons to his bedside.

"My sons," he said, "I will not be with you much longer, and I want you to know that I am leaving you something of great value in the vineyard, which will be yours when I die."

Not long afterward the farmer died. His sons soon set to work with spades and shovels turning over every inch of soil in the vineyard, hoping to find the treasure that lay buried there.

They found no treasure. But at the end of the season their painstaking plowing with spades and shovels had created a huge crop. The vines yielded a giant harvest of succulent grapes. As the sons pocketed the rich profit gained from their sale, they understood what their father had meant.

HARD WORK IS IN ITSELF A TREASURE.

THE STAG AND HIS REFLECTION

arly one morning a stag, drinking from a crystalline pool in the forest, noticed his reflection.

"What impressive antlers I have," he thought. "They are like the branches of a beautiful tree. But my legs are so thin and bony. I am not proud of them at all."

Just at that moment an arrow zinged past him. The stag realized that a hunter was no distance from him at all. He turned away from the pool and sprinted through the woods as fast as his legs could carry him. As he ran, his antlers became snagged on the branches of a tree. The stag was struggling to disentangle them when another arrow sped past him. In despair, he realized that he was trapped.

As he awaited his fate he thought, "How wrong I was to be critical of my legs. They might have saved me, except for my antlers."

VALUE SHOULD NOT BE MEASURED
BY APPEARANCES ALONE.

THE WOLF AND
THE CRANE

A wicked wolf was choking on a bone stuck deep in his throat. He was in terrible pain and, in desperation, promised a great reward to anyone who would take it out.

Knowing the greedy wolf very well, no one was very eager to help him. Finally the crane agreed to try.

With her long beak she was able to reach down the wolf's throat and get the bone out.

"Now, what will be my reward?" she said expectantly.

"Your reward, silly bird, is that you put your head inside a wolf's mouth and got it out safely. What more reward could you want?"

EXPECT NO REWARD WHEN YOU SERVE THE WICKED.

THE HARE AND THE TORTOISE

ne afternoon when he had nothing better to do, the fleet-footed hare was amusing himself by teasing his friend the tortoise about how slow he was. Imagine his amazement when the tortoise challenged *him* to a race!

"That's a ridiculous idea," the hare declared. "Think how embarrassing it will be for you."

The tortoise was not worried. The fox agreed to be the judge, and soon the competitors were off. The hare was out of sight in no time, while the tortoise plodded slowly along. Realizing that he could run the course at least twice in the time it took the tortoise to do it once, he settled down by a tree for a little nap.

Sometime later the hare awoke from his nap. He glanced behind him to see how much progress the tortoise had made, but the tortoise was nowhere in sight. He quickly pulled himself together and made a dash for the finish line, where the tortoise was waiting for him, looking very pleased with himself.

SLOW AND STEADY WINS THE RACE.

When to Tell a Story

Most parents like to tell stories at bedtime. For one thing, your child is about to step into the world of slumber and has slowed down; he is receptive, quiet, and focused. Generally you are too. You've already fought your battles of the day; you've moved through the joys and trials of the evening meal; you are ready for a refreshment of the spirit. Bedtime is an excellent time to tell a story, but it is not the only time.

- For the reluctant student, tell a tale in the car on the way to school.

- Gather all of the kids in your bed on Sunday morning and tell them a Bible story.

- Tell your two-year-old a story after lunch, when he is full and comfortable but not quite ready for a nap.

- Soothe your child with a helpful tale after he has had an awful experience on the playground or a run-in with other children.

- Give your sick child a hopeful tale about someone who fought and won.

- Use a holiday as an occasion to share a legend or a historical tale or a story about a saint.

Preparation for Reading

It stands to reason that a child who hears stories and tales will have a jump on reading when he goes to school. He'll have an adequate vocabulary to express his thoughts and should be well prepared to read and understand as well. Since comprehension is a crucial factor in learning to read, you can offer extra preparation for reading by encouraging your child to relate to ideas and information in the stories you share with him. From time to time, after you've told a story, ask him questions like these, based on "The Hare and the Tortoise":

1. Who was the judge in the race? (to check comprehension)
2. Why did the hare think he could nap during the race? (inference)

3. Do you think you would like to know the tortoise? (opinion).

You can help your child make the transition from hearing stories to reading them by occasionally writing or typing a story *he* tells *you*. This helps him to understand that printed material is similar to spoken language, and it helps to provide a basis for a strong written vocabulary.

Your child may enjoy hearing you read a story that you once told him. If he notices differences in the details, you can explain how stories vary with each teller or writer. Point out the similarities between music, where people can play the same song and have it sound different, and stories, where there may also be different interpretations.

THE FISHERMAN AND THE LITTLE FISH

nce upon a time, a fisherman who depended for his livelihood on what he caught in a day had one small fish in his net by sundown. The fish was remarkably vigorous and pleaded with the fisherman to let him go, saying, "I am so small, I am all but useless. Please throw me back and let me grow to my full size. Then you can catch me again and make a lot of money. You will not regret your decision."

The fisherman had the sense to say, "How can I give up what I have now for what I may or may not have tomorrow?"

A BIRD IN THE HAND
IS WORTH TWO IN THE BUSH.

THE BOY WHO CRIED WOLF

here once was a shepherd boy who watched his father's sheep every day in a pasture beside a deep, dark forest. The sheep did not need much attention, and the boy sometimes longed for a little excitement.

One day, just for fun, he called out, "Wolf! Wolf!" to see what would happen.

When they heard his cry, the villagers left their work and rushed to the pasture to help the boy. But when they got there, they saw no sign of a wolf. The shepherd boy laughed as he said, "There is no wolf. I just wanted to see what would happen if I called for help."

Several days later, when things seemed very quiet in the pasture, the shepherd boy played the same trick again. This time no one thought it was funny at all.

The very next day a wolf really did creep out of the pasture and start to chase the sheep.

"Wolf! Wolf!" the shepherd boy called out in terror. "Help! Help!" he cried, but no one paid any attention. The villagers looked at each other and shook their heads, thinking the shepherd boy was trying to trick them again.

There was not much left of the flock of sheep when the boy went home that day.

PEOPLE WILL NOT BELIEVE A LIAR,
EVEN WHEN HE'S TELLING THE TRUTH.

THE ANT AND THE DOVE

ne day an ant went to the bank of a stream to have a little drink of water. Much to her surprise, she found herself slipping into the spring.

Fortunately a dove was sitting on a branch over the stream and saw the ant fall in. Instantly she plucked a leaf off the branch near her and cast it into the stream. The leaf seemed like a life raft to the ant, who by now was struggling to stay afloat. The little ant clambered onto the raft gratefully and soon found her way to shore.

Just as the little ant found harbor, she looked up and noticed a hunter laying a trap for a bird. She was afraid that her friend the dove would be his victim.

Without hesitating a moment, the ant flew to the hunter and gave him a good sting in the foot.

With a cry of pain the hunter left his trap, giving fair warning to the dove of the danger. She lost no time in flying off to safety.

ONE ACT OF KINDNESS DESERVES ANOTHER.

THE FARMER'S DAUGHTER

ne sunny morning a farmer's daughter was carrying her pail back to the barn when she began day-dreaming.

"The money we get from this milk should buy twenty-five dozen eggs, and the eggs should produce about two hundred and fifty chickens. If all goes well, the chickens will fetch a good price at the market a few months hence."

She grew so excited, she could hardly think straight. "Perhaps by the end of the year," she thought, "I shall have enough money to buy a beautiful new dress. Then I shall go to a dance, and many handsome young men will want to marry me."

The farmer's daughter was just imagining how she would turn on her heel and walk away from the suitors who did not interest her when she lost her footing and let her milk pail fly down the path. She watched her dreams vanish as the milk flowed down the hill-side.

DON'T COUNT YOUR CHICKENS
BEFORE THEY'RE HATCHED.

THE FROG AND THE OX

here once was a big frog who lived in a small pond. He was the biggest creature in the pond and thought he was the biggest thing in the world. The smaller frogs in the pond would watch with envy as he sunned himself, puffing out his chest with pride.

One day three little frogs reported to the big frog that they had seen a terrible monster. They said he was as big as a mountain and had horns and a tail and hooves. Soon after that this creature, the ox, came to drink at the pond. The big frog was intent on impressing him.

"You are pretty tall," the frog allowed, "but I can make myself as broad as you." The ox was not listening. He just kept drinking.

The frog started to huff and puff and blow himself out. The ox paid no attention.

Soon the frog had inflated himself to twice his usual size. "What do you think of that?" he called out breathlessly.

The ox did not even notice. He had finished drinking and was walking away from the pond.

This made the frog so furious that he took an enormous breath. He grew so round, he didn't look like a frog anymore. "Am I as big as the ox?" he asked in a weak voice.

Then the only sound on the pond was a big *pop!*

WE SHOULD NOT TRY TO BE WHAT WE ARE NOT.

THE CROW AND
THE PITCHER

crow was nearly dying of thirst when he came upon a tall pitcher, half full of cool, clear water. The crow leaned eagerly into the pitcher for a refreshing drink. But his beak was not long enough to reach the water. The crow was nearly wild with frustration until he thought what to do.

Beneath the windowsill where the pitcher stood were some pebbles lying on the ground. The crow flew down and picked up as many as he could carry. One by one he dropped the pebbles into the pitcher. Each time the level of the water rose a little higher. After many trips back and forth the crow had many pebbles. By the time he had dropped them all into the pitcher, the water nearly reached the top. The crow was then able to drink his fill.

WITH A LITTLE EFFORT YOU CAN GET WHAT YOU
WANT.

THE FOX AND THE STORK

nce, long ago, when the fox and the stork were getting along well, the fox invited the stork to dinner. As a joke, the fox served nothing but soup in a very shallow dish. The fox lapped up his share of the soup quickly while the stork sat staring at her plate; her bill was so long that she could not possibly drink the soup, and she left the table as hungry as when she sat down.

"I'm sorry you didn't care for the soup," said the fox rather slyly.

"Oh, that's all right," said the stork politely. "I look forward to having you dine with me soon."

A week or so later the stork invited the fox for dinner. The fox was somewhat dismayed when he sat down to eat. His dinner was contained in a tubelike jar with a narrow opening at the top. The fox could fit only enough of his snout in the opening to smell the delicious food that was at the bottom. The stork ate as if everything were perfectly normal while the fox sniffed and occasionally licked the outside of the strange container.

Later, as the fox was about to depart looking very disappointed, the stork said sweetly, "I trust I need not feel guilty about the meal."

A JOKE IS NOT AS AMUSING
WHEN YOU ARE ITS VICTIM.

THE WOLF AND
THE LAMB

 wolf was drinking at a brook when he caught sight of a woolly lamb wading farther downstream. The wolf was hungry and wanted to eat the lamb for lunch. He thought to himself how he might justify such a violent deed.

He bounded up to the bank of the stream beside her. "How dare you muddy the water that I drink?" he charged.

"How could I possibly be muddying the water you drink," replied the lamb, "when you drink way upstream from me?"

"Harumpf," the wolf snorted as he quickly tried to think of something else to blame on her. "I still remember all those ugly names you called me a year ago."

"That's impossible," said the little lamb weakly. "I wasn't even born a year ago."

"Well, it was your father, then," said the wolf, "and that's just as bad." And with that he leapt upon the helpless little lamb and gobbled her all up.

EXCUSES COME EASILY
TO THOSE WHO DO EVIL.

Homegrown Tales

From time to time you will want to create a make-believe story, an adventure all your own that simply "happens." Here are some guidelines for better spontaneous storytelling.

- Create a character or two that can go through a series of mishaps or ordeals or happy events. If you plan on using this character often, you do not need to elaborate on his character too much, as he will reveal himself by the action he takes in different situations. Many parents have created a mythical character and have used him as an unofficial family member who pops up in letters and notes and even birthday cards.

- Frame your story with a good beginning and ending, just as you would the most formal of tales. At the least, start with *once upon a time.* You might even want to start a trademark beginning or ending, as many professional storytellers have.

- If you are making up a story, you can meet your audience more than halfway. Ask your child if he wants to hear an adventure story, a funny story, or a slow, sad story. You will be surprised at the powerful effect a story can have when it matches moods.

- Let your tale flow from you. Relax and follow your imagination. Listen to your words. Imagine a scene and tell your child what you see. The story is playing in your mind; you just have to tell what you are seeing.

- If you had fun telling it, your child may want to hear the story again. In this case you've got a hit on your hands and you should not let it go. Write down the story as you can best recollect it. Fine-tune it. Tell it again a week later. You have created something that could last for generations if you take care of it.

- If you are stumped for a subject or unable to get the plot moving, try thinking of a provocative title for your story before you tell it. Put yourself in the position of explaining "why God gave us ears." Set up a situation where two people are vying for the same thing but for different reasons. Fix on an item in your child's room and weave a tale about how it got there.

- Some parents like to involve their children in telling tales, and this can work most effectively if you are sincere about it. Ask your child to cheer you up by telling you a happy story. If you have a group of children, have them all participate in the creation of a story by directing them: "And then what happened, Patrick?" This kind of play aids immeasurably in the development of their imaginative, conceptual, and language skills.

THE MARRIAGE
OF THE SUN

here once was a time, during a very hot summer, when the animals learned that the sun was going to be married. At first there was great celebration, until a wise old frog pointed out that the sun's marriage could cause problems. "Consider how the sun dries up our beautiful marshes now," he said. "What will become of us when he has children and there are many more suns to parch the land?"

IT IS POSSIBLE TO HAVE
TOO MUCH OF A GOOD THING.

THE BUNDLE OF STICKS

father had four sons who argued with each other constantly. The father loved his sons, and he knew they loved each other, but he was concerned about the time and energy they wasted by fighting so much. He set his mind to finding some way to show them how foolish this was.

One day, when they were together, the father picked up a bundle of sticks. He asked who thought he could break the bundle in two.

Each boy tried to do it, but not one succeeded. After all four had failed, the father calmly untied the bundle and gave each son a stick. "Now," he said, "show me how you can break that in two."

The sons snapped the sticks in half with scarcely any effort at all.

"Do you understand now?" he asked. "On your own, each of you is weak. Together you are as strong as the bundle of sticks. You should not allow arguing to pull you apart."

THOSE WHO STAND TOGETHER ARE STRONGER
THAN THOSE WHO STAND APART.

THE LION AND
THE MOUSE

ne hot summer day a lion lay basking sleepily in the sun. A brazen little mouse challenged himself to run over the lion's nose without rousing him. Just when he thought he'd made it safely, the lion awakened and caught the mouse. He was about to swat him with his paw when the mouse pleaded, "Please forgive me. If you will just let me go, I'll do something equally kind for you someday."

The lion was very amused by that idea. He admired the mouse's impudence enough that he decided to let the little creature go.

Not long after that the lion found himself caught in a hunter's net. The mouse heard him roaring with anger and scurried to see what was wrong.

He found the lion thrashing pathetically in the hunter's net. Without a word the mouse set himself to gnawing a hole in the net big enough for the lion to escape.

"You see," said the mouse, "you laughed when I said I would repay your kindness one day. And so I have."

The lion was pleased to admit that this was true.

NEVER UNDERESTIMATE THE VALUE OF KINDNESS.

THE LION, THE FOX, AND THE ASS

he lion, the fox, and the ass once joined in a hunt together and agreed to share the spoils afterward. When it was over, the lion very generously asked the ass to work out the portions due each of them. The ass took great pains to divide the portions evenly, then asked his companions to choose the ones they wanted.

His eyes flaring with rage, the lion delivered a mighty blow of his paw to the ass and killed him instantly. Then the lion asked the fox to divide the spoils again. The fox piled all the booty into one large heap, except for a small morsel, which he set aside for himself.

The lion looked pleased. "I like the way you did that," he said. "That's what I call a fair division of the spoils. How do you come by such talent?"

"I learned it from the ass," replied the fox very humbly.

HE WHO LEARNS FROM OTHERS
SAVES HIMSELF THEIR MISFORTUNE.

THE BEAR AND THE TRAVELERS

Once, long ago, two young men were traveling together through a forest. Suddenly a big bear came crashing out of the woods behind them.

One of the young men quickly grabbed hold of a low branch and swung himself to safety.

The other young man saw no such opportunity to save himself, so he flung himself on the ground as if he were dead. He knew that a bear will not touch a dead body.

The bear approached the young man on the ground and sniffed him well before he trundled off with a growl.

The young man in the tree finally came down. "It looked as if that bear were whispering to you," he said. "What did he say?"

"He said," replied his companion, "that it's not a very good idea to travel with someone who will desert you in a difficult situation."

MISFORTUNE IS A TEST OF TRUE FRIENDSHIP.

THE GOOSE THAT LAID THE GOLDEN EGG

ne day, to his great amazement, a farmer discovered that his old gray goose had laid an egg that was pure gold.

"Look at this!" he called to his wife. "Our gray goose has laid a golden egg!"

Imagine the farmer's excitement when, the next day, he found that the goose had laid another golden egg. And each day he found another.

Although the farmer soon had a basketful of golden eggs, he became greedy. "I want all the goose's golden eggs," he told his wife. "They'll be worth a fortune."

Against his wife's advice he cut the bird open but found not one egg inside. He would never have a fortune, and he'd lost his good gray goose.

**HE WHO IS TOO GREEDY
MAY END UP WITH NOTHING.**

ANDROCLES AND THE LION

slave named Androcles was so tormented by his master that he escaped from him and hid in the forest. He had not been there long when he came upon a lion who was moaning loudly. He was about to run away when he saw that the lion was groaning because he was in terrible pain. There was a thorn stuck in his paw, which was bleeding and swollen.

Androcles could see from the expression in the lion's eyes that the poor creature desperately wanted some help. He took the lion's paw in his own hands and very gently drew out the thorn. The lion licked Androcles' hand gratefully and hobbled off into the woods.

A few days later both Androcles and the lion were captured by Roman soldiers. As punishment for running away, Androcles was sentenced to be thrown to the lion, who was kept without food for three days.

The emperor, his court, and all of Rome were invited to see the hungry lion tear the runaway slave limb from limb. Released from the cage where he'd been held captive, the lion bounded into the ring, wild with anger and hunger. But when he saw Androcles, he trotted over to him and licked his hands and face like a puppy dog. The emperor summoned Androcles to him, who told him the story of the lion and his sore paw. The emperor was so impressed that Androcles was freed, and the lion was taken back to live in peace in the forest.

GRATITUDE IS THE SIGN OF A NOBLE SOUL

THE FOX AND THE GOAT

arly one morning a fox was ambling along, not looking where he was going. Before he knew it, he'd lost his footing and fallen down a well. The fox could not think how to get out.

Some time later a goat came by looking for a drink of water.

"The water down here is great," called out the fox.

The goat figured that if the fox had gone down there to drink, why shouldn't he? He jumped in without hesitating.

The fox quickly leapt on his back, set one foot on each of the goat's horns, and pulled himself out of the well.

"Now how do I get out?" yelled the goat.

"You should have thought of that before," said the fox with a laugh as he went on his way, leaving the goat behind.

LOOK BEFORE YOU LEAP.

THE MICE IN COUNCIL

any years ago the mice held a meeting to decide what to do about the cat that was making their lives miserable. All of the mice came to the meeting, but none of them could think of a plan that had not been tried before and failed.

Then a young mouse stood up to propose his idea.

"Obviously," he began, "the trouble with the cat is that he is quiet and sly and can sneak up on us without our knowing it."

That, they agreed, was the problem.

"What we have to do," the young mouse went on confidently, "is get a small bell and put it around the cat's neck. Then we'll know where the cat is and what he is doing at all times."

The mice responded warmly to this suggestion and began whispering to each other about the clever young mouse who had proposed it. Then the oldest and wisest mouse rose from his seat and said, "The young mouse has certainly made a brilliant suggestion, but who among us is going to risk his neck to put the bell on the cat?"

IDEAS THAT CANNOT BE EXECUTED HAVE LITTLE MERIT.

What to Tell When

For the most part, common sense will guide you in selecting stories to tell to your child. Age, in this case, is less a factor than your child's particular stage of development. These stages represent a variety of skills, including his ability to imagine, visualize, and focus. Experience also plays an important role in determining how "ready" your child is for a certain kind of tale.

You can start at day one. Even a newborn will appreciate a rhythmical, repetitive story (and, of course, nursery rhymes). Your child obviously has a limited vocabulary (or no vocabulary at all), but he can benefit from hearing your voice in what will seem to him a structured, deliberate presentation. Stories like "The Little Red Hen" ("Not I," said the goose. "Not I," said the cat. "Not I," said the pig.) and "The Gingerbread Boy" ("Run, run, as fast as you can, you can't catch me, I'm the Gingerbread Man.") are perfect fare.

From the age of two, your child will be ready for simple plots. At this point I recommend the "three" tales: "The Three Billy Goats Gruff," "The Three Bears," and "The Three Little Pigs." These stories really tickle children, and even though your child may not be able to understand all of the words, he will be able to grasp the story line. Do not be afraid to use words your child is unfamiliar with from time to time; he can comprehend much more than you think—and he will be absorbing a sense of grammar at the very least.

Romances are next; these are my favorites. Here you can share the extraordinary adventures of "Cinderella," "Snow White," "Jack and the Beanstalk," "Hansel and Gretel," and so on. The plots are more complicated, the characters are more meaningful, and the dire straits (fleeing from ogres and witches and mean stepsisters) are the best. If you have reservations about the psychological impact of a certain story, you can submit it to a simple test. For example, if you are worried about "Little Red Riding Hood," ask yourself the most important question: Has your child ever ventured out on his own? Has he ever gone to a relative's home by himself? If he has had some experience out on his own, he will know that a walk into the world won't necessarily result in his becoming wolf bait. Therefore you can relax. These stories have not lasted hundreds of years because they are dangerous.

Between the ages of two and five, stories can serve as an interesting measuring stick for intellectual development. However subjective an experiment it is, you might try, as legendary storyteller Marie Shedlock suggests, to tell the same story to your child at six-month intervals. After each telling, talk to your child about the story and be aware of his questions or the emphasis he places on certain characters or events. You will be amazed at how his grasp of the story so truly reflects his grasp of language and of life itself.

The most exciting time for storytelling is between ages five and nine. Your child is learning to read (or reading voraciously) at this point, and your storytelling efforts not only promote the intrinsic value of a good tale but help him to develop his language skills. At this point you are telling romance tales, as well as fables and myths and legends. Fables are very sophisticated stories, and it is important for your child to have had some world experience, especially experience with other children, before you begin to tell them. Myths and legends also require a more sophisticated child.

These guidelines hold true for most children, but remember that you can never really tell a story that is over your child's head. If you have more than one child, do not reduce your telling to the lowest common denominator. Children understand more than you think. If *you* understand the essence of your story, your child will, too.

THE CITY MOUSE AND THE COUNTRY MOUSE

ne day the city mouse decided to visit her cousin who lived in the country. Her country cousin was pleased to see her and welcomed her warmly. She considered the visit such a special occasion that she put together a meal of the best of everything she had in the house. It was only a few bits of cheese and bacon, but the country mouse presented these with pride to her guest.

The country mouse enjoyed the treats she had set out, but the city mouse scarcely touched her meal. She was used to fancier things. Finally the city mouse said, "Cousin, how can you bear to live like this? Your life is so dull and boring. Come with me and I will show you what you have been missing."

The country mouse was quite content with her life, but she agreed to go with her cousin and they went off together.

Late the same night the two mice arrived at the town house where the city mouse lived. "Follow me," she said, and she led her cousin into the dining room where the remains of a fine feast were scattered about the table. The country mouse scampered behind her city cousin, sampling a little bit of everything. She could hardly believe the wonders that lay before her—cranberry sauce, choco-late-covered mints, all manner of cheeses and fruits.

"How I have wasted my time in the country," she thought, "when I could live like this. This is heaven!"

Just then the doors of the dining room were flung open, and in came the servants and their friends to enjoy the leftovers of the feast too. Afraid for their lives, the mice flew from the table to the nearest hiding place and waited until the people went away. Just as they were about to venture out again, a large dog came bounding into the room, pulling at the tablecloth to get his share of the goodies.

When the dog went away and things seemed to have quieted down for good, the country mouse left her hiding place, eager to say good-bye to her cousin and return to the country. "You're welcome to city life, dear cousin, but it's not for me. I would far rather eat simply in the country than feast like this, not knowing what will happen next."

A SIMPLE LIFE LIVED IN PEACE IS PREFERABLE TO A LUXURIOUS LIFE LIVED IN FEAR.

The Best Characters Are in Your Own Backyard

As a new parent, you are not only a storyteller and a singer but the custodian of your family history, a very important role, indeed. These real-life stories not only make for splendid entertainment but for a marvelous personal oral tradition, one that you will value more over time.

As with any story you tell, your family histories must have a beginning, a middle, and an end. They can be as short as a long joke or as long as a short story, but they must follow the curve of the tale. Pull your histories out of their anecdotal form and give them the presence and life of a story.

Finding a family history is not difficult. Almost every family I know has a tale of their lost or squandered fortune (why we are not rich) or a tale of their grandfather walking miles to school in terrible weather (why we are not grandfather). My husband, I noticed, has been polishing up his most devastating childhood tale: the true story of Great Aunt Hazel of Groesbeck, Texas, who in 1897 received a stocking filled with nothing but ugly black switches on Christmas morning, the result, it seems, of bad behavior. Though many years have passed since Aunt Hazel's awful Christmas morn, the story still packs an awesome punch for little children, especially when told around mid-December.

When you are looking for family stories, don't overlook tales about eccentric relatives; every family has one real standout. War stories are a superb source. So is every family's how-we-got-to-America story.

The best stories of all, though, are the family romance stories, especially "How Mom and Dad Met." My father loves to recount his days at the University of Minnesota, sitting in a stuffy, dull French class. Every Tuesday morning a beautiful, graceful woman would pass mysteriously by his window, promptly at eleven. One day, as the semester was about to end, he could take the suspense no longer. He jumped up from his desk, dashed out of the room, and presented himself most clumsily to the startled young woman. Three years later she became his wife.

The key to preserving your family histories is to approach them as a true chronicler of times and places and characters. Do your homework, especially if you were not there. Use family gatherings to get the facts, the details, the different sides of the story. Keep a notebook of ideas and insights. Incorporate little flashes of color: the dress she wore, the price of ginger ale, the election year, hair styles. Look for emotions in your stories: sadness, surprise, joy, awe. If there are lessons to be learned, by all means share them. This is the start of your family's "folk wisdom." And it is one of those rare gifts only you can give your children.

THE FOX AND THE CROW

ne bright summer morning a big black crow found a lovely piece of cheese left behind by some picnickers in the woods. She flew to the branch of a tree with it in her beak and was looking forward to eating it when a clever fox passed by below her.

"Hmmmm," said the clever fox, "wouldn't that piece of cheese taste good for my breakfast. But how can I get it without frightening the crow away?"

Soon he had a scheme. "Good morning, crow," he said in his most sugary voice. "How well you are looking today. I never realized what an elegant creature you are."

The crow did not open her mouth. The fox went on.

"How beautiful your feathers are when they catch the sun like that. Tell me, do you sing sweetly too?"

The crow hesitated only a moment. Dizzy with joy from all this flattery, she could not resist demonstrating her voice with a loud "Caw."

As soon as she opened her beak, the cheese dropped right into the fox's mouth.

"Thank you for the cheese," the fox said in parting. "And beware of flatterers. You're lucky you only lost a little piece of cheese."

BE WARY OF FALSE PRAISE.

THE FARMER, THE SON, AND THE DONKEY

ne day a farmer and his son decided that it was time to take their donkey to market. He had grown fat and sturdy, and they felt sure they could get a good price for him.

They had barely started out when they passed a group of young girls tittering to themselves.

"Aren't they ridiculous?" the farmer heard one girl say. "Why would anyone trudge along beside a donkey when they could be riding?"

The farmer could not help but agree. He told his son to climb on the donkey.

They had not gone far when they passed a group of farmers leaning on a fence and talking.

"Imagine that!" the son heard one of them say. "That disrespectful young man is content to ride in comfort while his father walks."

The son hopped down from the donkey immediately and urged his father to take his place. About twenty yards down the road they came across a few old ladies chatting among themselves. As they drew close, several of the women called out, "You heartless old man! Why do you ride in style while your little boy runs along trying to keep up with you? He'll be exhausted by the time you get to the village."

The farmer had not thought of that. Right away he pulled his son up onto the donkey with him, and they rode along together.

By now they were getting close to the market. A villager who was also headed that way called out to the farmer.

"Hey," he said, "is that your donkey?"

"Yes," replied the farmer.

The villager turned to the other people in the street. "Would you believe it?" he said. "Look how that man has that poor beast loaded down."

The good-natured farmer had not intended to abuse his donkey. He and his son climbed off the donkey's back and set their minds to figuring out how they could carry the donkey. They asked a shopkeeper if they could borrow a broomstick, and with some rope that they found nearby they tied both pairs of the donkey's feet to the pole. The donkey complained bitterly and did his best to get free, but the farmer and his son finally managed to lift the broomstick, bearing the donkey to their shoulders. On they went, toward the town bridge, with villagers hooting and hollering at them as they passed. The donkey, making his share of noise, too, finally succeeded in kicking himself free, but he was so dizzy by then that he tumbled off the bridge into the water. Alas, he could not swim and soon drowned.

The farmer and the son, thinking it was all their fault, went home empty-handed.

IF YOU TRY TO PLEASE EVERYONE,
YOU RISK PLEASING NO ONE.

THE WOLF AND THE KID

ne day a young kid wandered away from the other goats and found himself alone in a meadow. To his horror he realized that a wolf had seen him and was coming after him. He ran as hard as he could, then, as the wolf came near, he said, "All right, wolf, I know I can't run away from you. You're much faster than I am. But if you must eat me, will you grant me one favor? Will you play me a tune on your little pipe so that I may have a few minutes of joy before I die?"

The wolf agreed, and the kid danced on his hind legs as a lilting tune was played. Some distance away, the dogs heard the music and grew curious. They ran to the meadow to see who was playing the music. The minute the wolf saw the dogs coming toward him, he was gone in a flash, leaving the kid unharmed.

**THINGS ARE NOT ALWAYS
AS BLEAK AS THEY SEEM.**

THE FOX AND THE GRAPES

ne fine fall afternoon a fox was running through a field when he caught sight of a bunch of ripe grapes hanging on a vine that trailed from the branch of an old tree. The grapes were purple and bursting with juice.

The fox licked his lips. "These grapes will surely quench my thirst," he thought.

He then leaned back on his haunches and jumped high in the air but missed the grapes by a hair. He tried taking a running jump from the other direction but missed once more. Again and again he attempted to reach the luscious grapes and failed. Finally the fox became exhausted and couldn't jump anymore. He walked away muttering to himself, "Who would want those grapes, anyway. I am sure they are sour."

IT IS EASY TO HAVE CONTEMPT FOR SOMETHING YOU CANNOT OBTAIN.

CHAPTER FOUR

Songs

"Awake and sing."
—Isaiah 26:19

INTRODUCTION

One morning when I was impatiently trying to stuff my daughter's foot into a walking shoe (Shoe Wars, as we call them), I handed her a tiny music box, thinking it a masterstroke of diversion. Her fingers fumbled at first, but once she got it going, *Eine kleine Nachtmusik* began pouring out merrily, accompanied by the sweetest humming I have ever heard. At sixteen months, Virginia was singing to Mozart and in utter earnest.

I suppose some battles are worth losing.

Children can actually sing before they speak, whether it is a lazy babble or a brightly wielded melody. This is due in part to the fact that music and language are stored in two different parts of the brain. Leonard Bernstein has averred that all babies are born with a universal song on their lips, the Ur-Song, as it is called. *(Ur* is the German prefix that means primeval or universal.) Cosmic melody or no, every parent knows no finer sound than that of his own child busy at song.

The songs that I have gathered in this section aspire to one thing and one thing only: fun. They are adamantly traditional, corny, old-fashioned, and all of those things that (in the final analysis) endure. To my way of thinking, the person who does not know the words and the music to "Oh Dear, What Can the Matter Be" is not merely deprived but, in a certain way, uneducated. These songs are part of our cultural heritage. They are now yours to share and enjoy for years to come.

Singing, for most of us, is something we do in showers, on Sunday mornings, or in furtive bits as we race down the highway listening to the radio. Most of us are not natural performers until that first child arrives. Upon his arrival, we become slightly mad crooners. Children do that to us for many reasons but mainly because they make us happy.

Now, as newcomers to the singing stage, we must be comforted by the fact that the quality of our voices (and this from recent studies) has no effect whatsoever on our children's appreciation for music. It is quite true that depriving your child of music early in life can have a devastating effect on his affinity and talent for music, but off-key notes and a lousy range are just as compelling to the child's musical imagination as the most perfectly wrought aria. The point is that you sing—period. This is not a point to be taken lightly if your child's musical education is of any concern at all. The love and aptitude for music is decidedly born in the very first three years, and it would be silly to deprive your child of this. So do not be shy.

Those of us without musical training can follow a simple piece of advice: Sing from just below your waist, not from your throat. Pull your notes from down deep and your voice is more likely to settle on the right notes, your breathing will be more natural, and you won't sound like an extra from *The Wizard of Oz.*

Just as in the case of storytelling, singing must be a heralded event, not just background material, like some sort of homegrown Muzak. Researchers show that flooding a child with music doesn't work. Do not let your radio drone on and on all day long. When you do play the radio or a record, make it an occasion. If you are singing, make sure your child is aware that you are having a jolly good time (and don't sing if you aren't). Use exaggerated facial expressions. Sing with your eyes.

If you can, develop a set of rituals that incorporate your favorite songs. You might begin each day with "Frère Jacques" or sing "Oh Where, Oh Where Has My Little Dog Gone?" when you take your pooch out for his constitutional. Take the time to review the different lyrics in this book and sing a new and different song to your child whenever you think of it. You will discover that your child will "take" to a couple of songs in particular, and you can sing them to your heart's content to an always ready audience.

I confessed earlier that I am a bit of a snob, and snobs do quite poorly as parents who want to share the gift of music. This is not a time for narrow tastes. You should allow your child to be exposed to endlessly diverse fare, from rock and roll to country to classical to jazz and kid's music. (I suppose you could skip over certain polkas.) The most important thing is to make sure your children experience listening to "good" music as well as the more frivolous genres. For them, music is a physical sensation, not just a spiritual migration. Let them boogy, get down, and do whatever. They are building a musical vocabulary that must be as broad as it is deep.

The guiding principle we must apply to both singing and playing musical instruments is, as we have said before and many times, *make it fun.* Just as children will be drawn to the language because they experience its powers in a well-told story, the power of a happily sung song or a perfectly plucked guitar can bring children into the extraordinary world of music. Your voice, what it says and tells and sings, is the most powerful force in your child's first years. Let it sing in a way that shows you are gloriously alive.

BILLY BOY

Oh, where are you going,
Billy Boy, Billy Boy?
Oh, where are you going,
Charming Billy?
I am going to see my wife,
She's the joy of my life,
She's a young thing and cannot leave her mother.

Can she make a cherry pie,
Billy Boy, Billy Boy?
Can she make a cherry pie,
Charming Billy?
She can make a cherry pie,
Quick as a cat can wink its eye,
She's a young thing and cannot leave her mother.

POP! GOES THE WEASEL

All around the cobbler's bench,
The monkey chased the weasel,
The monkey thought 'twas all in fun.
Pop! goes the weasel.

A penny for a spool of thread,
A penny for a needle,
That's the way the money goes,
Pop! goes the weasel.

LAZY MARY

Lazy Mary, will you get up,
Will you get up, will you get up?
Lazy Mary, will you get up,
Will you get up today?

No, no, Mother, I won't get up,
I won't get up, I won't get up,
No, no, Mother, I won't get up,
I won't get up today.

Instruments You Can Make

As soon as he is two years old, almost any child can play an instrument on his own. Pots and wooden spoons are fine for beating out basic rhythms, and when he is ready to produce a greater variety of sounds, there are many simple instruments you can make at home. Be sure all materials you use are nontoxic, and also be careful not to leave any rough edges, nails, or sharp points.

Drums can be made from round boxes or tubes. Cover the open ends with a piece of rubber, parchment, or adhesive-backed plastic. Secure the covering with a rubber band or string. Decorate with colored paper, glued-on cord, ribbon, or braid. Remember that a small drum will have a soft, relatively high tone; a large drum will produce a lower, more clunky sound.

For **rattles** use a variety of small containers that you have around the house. Plastic storage containers work well. So do empty spice jars. Anything that has a tightly fastened lid will do. Fill the containers with rice, buttons, pebbles, beads, marbles. Each of these will produce a different sound.

To make **rhythm sticks** start with lengths of wooden doweling cut six to eight inches long, one half to one inch in diameter. These make perfectly good drumsticks and can be used for hitting tone blocks or resonator bells. By the time your child is two years old, he can use full-size rhythm sticks, twelve to thirteen inches long and one half to three inches in diameter.

A small **cowbell** is a good instrument for a child, or if that's too noisy, sew small bells onto a wristband or handle that can be waved around.

BLUE-TAIL FLY
(JIMMIE CRACK CORN)

When I was young I used to wait
On my master and give him his plate,
And pass the bottle when he got dry,
And brush away the blue-tail fly.

CHORUS:

Jimmie crack corn and I don't care,
Jimmie crack corn and I don't care,
Jimmie crack corn and I don't care,
My master's gone away.

And when he'd ride in the afternoon,
I'd follow after with a hickory broom,
The pony being rather shy
When bitten by a blue-tail fly.

CHORUS

One day he rode around the farm;
The flies so numerous, they did swarm;
One chanced to bite him in the thigh;
The devil take the blue-tail fly.

CHORUS

The pony run, he jump, he pitch,
He threw my master in the ditch.
He died, and the jury wondered why.
The verdict was the blue-tail fly.

CHORUS

They lay him under a 'simmon tree;
His epitaph is there to see:
"Beneath this stone I'm forced to lie,
A victim of the blue-tail fly."

CHORUS

ROLL OVER

There were ten in the bed
And the little one said,
"Roll over, roll over."
So they all rolled over
And one fell out. . . .

There were
nine in the bed
And the little one said,
"Roll over, roll over."
So they all rolled over
And one fell out. . . .

There were
eight in the bed
And the little one said,
"Roll over, roll over."
So they all rolled over
And one fell out. . . .

There were
seven in the bed
And the little one said,
"Roll over, roll over."
So they all rolled over
And one fell out. . . .

There were
six in the bed
And the little one said,
"Roll over, roll over."
So they all rolled over
And one fell out. . . .

There were
five in the bed
And the little one said,
"Roll over, roll over."
So they all rolled over
And one fell out. . . .

There were
four in the bed
And the little one said,
"Roll over, roll over."

Musical Milestones

By the time a child is five years old, he can truly sing a song. But the road to that first fully vocalized song is a long, though fascinating, one. Harvard's Project Zero, which studies artistic thinking, examined the musical development of children up to five years old and released its findings a few years ago. Here are some of the highlights:

- Children spend the first eighteen months in a period of wide-reaching experimentation. What we perceive as rather cute babble and cooing is actually an exploration process that is melodic and intonational, as well as phonological. In fact, the first year of babbling is in many ways more about song than speech. Many infants at this age are able to roughly approximate a pitch; they are sensitive enough to the fact that there is such a thing as pitch to want to mimic it.

- At eighteen months children can intentionally produce a pitch. As words start to enter their repertoire, their ability to sing increases. By two and a half years, children have, for the first time, an explicit awareness of tunes sung by others. Their vocabulary has developed to the point that they can match their pitch to the words and reproduce the words in a more controlled way with what the researchers described as spontaneous song, which is basically melodic bits and pieces. This stage combines the spontaneous singing with the lyrics, and a song begins to emerge.

- At three years old children can sing what researchers called "learned song." They have mastered the rhythmic structure of a song and have combined the segments they are familiar with (rhythm and words and basic pitch) into one almost identifiable piece. They have not really targeted in on the song, but they are very close.

- From three to four years children have a true grasp of song for the first time. They still lack key and tonality, but if they hummed it without the benefit of lyrics (which they use to help maintain rhythm), you would be able to identify it. A four-year-old can learn the words, the surface rhythm of the song, and the contour of the song (when it goes up and down and for how long).

- At five years children can beat time at regular intervals. They can sing a song. In the first five years they have covered almost every aspect of musical development that there is to cover and, when tested against an adult, will compare favorably in the mastery of a new song. The singing that they do in their future years will only be practice and refinement of the skills they learned before the age of five.

The Right Stuff

If you were not blessed with a gorgeous voice, you will be interested to know that the critical difference between haves and have-nots has nothing to do with willpower. As it happens, our voices, control over their hands and all of the smaller muscles.

It is the ability to control these small muscles that sets the musician apart.

In many ways the musician is graced with the same muscular control as the athlete, although the athlete is given control of the larger muscles. In both cases physical advantages are accompanied by strenuous exercise and relentless practice. Thus behavioral tendencies—especially an acceptance of discipline—also figure in the making of a superb tenor or a great pianist.

If your child exhibits an interest in singing or playing an instrument, your encouragement, support, and a patient ear will play a major role in the development of his particular genius. If perhaps you do not have a Van Cliburn and your child is frustrated or bored with the process, support him with whimsy and fun rather than the specter of achievement. Those of us who have been graced with the ability to hear have, at the least, the chance to be what a famed American composer calls the "gifted listener." Keep the joy of music alive for your child. As Aaron Copland put it, "Listening is its own reward . . . there are few pleasures in art greater than the sense that one can recognize beauty when one comes upon it." Your commitment to understanding and appreciating the beauty of music will make the difference in how your child "hears the world."

So they all rolled over
And one fell out. . . .

There were
three in the bed
And the little one said,
"Roll over, roll over."
So they all rolled over
And one fell out. . . .

There were
two in the bed
And the little one said,
"Roll over, roll over."
So they all rolled over
And one fell out. . . .

There was
one in the bed
And the little one said,
(spoken) "Good night."

GO TELL AUNT RHODY

Go tell Aunt Rhody,
Go tell Aunt Rhody,
Go tell Aunt Rhody,
Her old gray goose is dead.

The one she's been saving,
The one she's been saving,
The one she's been saving,
To make a feather bed.

She died in the millpond,
She died in the millpond,
She died in the millpond,
Standing on her head.

I'VE BEEN WORKING ON THE RAILROAD

I've been working on the railroad,
  All the live-long day,
I've been working on the railroad,
  Just to pass the time away.
Don't you hear the whistle blowing,
  Rise up so early in the morn.
Don't you hear the captain shouting,
  Dinah, blow your horn!

Dinah, won't you blow,
Dinah, won't you blow,
Dinah, won't you blow your horn?
Dinah, won't you blow,
Dinah, won't you blow,
Dinah, won't you blow your horn?

Someone's in the kitchen with Dinah,
Someone's in the kitchen I know,
Someone's in the kitchen with Dinah,
Strummin' on the old banjo.

Fee, Fie, Fiddle-ee-i-o,
Fee, Fie, Fiddle-ee-i-o,
Fee, Fie, Fiddle-ee-i-o,
Strummin' on the old banjo.

FRÈRE JACQUES

Frère Jacques, Frère Jacques,
Dormez-vous? Dormez-vous?
Sonnez les matines,
Sonnez les matines,
Din, dan, don,
Din, dan, don.

ENGLISH TRANSLATION

Are you sleeping, are you sleeping,
Brother John? Brother John?
Morning bells are ringing,
Morning bells are ringing,
Ding, dong, ding,
Ding, dong, ding.

SHOO, FLY, DON'T BOTHER ME

Shoo, fly, don't bother me,
Shoo, fly, don't bother me,
Shoo, fly, don't bother me,
For I belong to somebody.
I feel, I feel, I feel like a morning star,
I feel, I feel, I feel like a morning star.
So shoo, fly, don't bother me,
Shoo, fly, don't bother me,
Shoo, fly, don't bother me,
For I belong to somebody.

SKIP TO MY LOU

Skip, skip, skip to my lou,
Skip, skip, skip to my lou,
Skip, skip, skip to my lou,
Skip to my lou, my darling.

Lost my partner, what'll I do?
Lost my partner, what'll I do?
Lost my partner, what'll I do?
Skip to my lou, my darling.

I'll find another one, prettier too.
I'll find another one, prettier too.
I'll find another one, prettier too.
Skip to my lou, my darling.

Flies in the buttermilk, shoo, fly, shoo.
Flies in the buttermilk, shoo, fly, shoo.
Flies in the buttermilk, shoo, fly, shoo.
Skip to my lou, my darling.

FROGGIE WENT A-COURTIN'

Froggie went a-courtin' and he did ride (mm-hmm, mm-hmm),
Froggie went a-courtin' and he did ride (mm-hmm, mm-hmm),
Froggie went a-courtin' and he did ride,
Sword and pistol by his side, (mm-hmm, mm-hmm)!

Rode up to Miss Mousey's door (mm-hmm, mm-hmm),
Rode up to Miss Mousey's door (mm-hmm, mm-hmm),
Rode up to Miss Mousey's door,
Where he'd often been before (mm-hmm, mm-hmm)!

Said, Miss Mousey, are you within (mm-hmm, mm-hmm),
Said, Miss Mousey, are you within (mm-hmm, mm-hmm),
Said, Miss Mousey, are you within?
Yes, kind sir, I sit and spin (mm-hmm, mm-hmm)!

Took Miss Mousey on his knee (mm-hmm, mm-hmm),
Took Miss Mousey on his knee (mm-hmm, mm-hmm),
Took Miss Mousey on his knee,
Said Miss Mousey, will you marry me? (mm-hmm, mm-hmm)!

Without my Uncle Rat's consent (mm-hmm, mm-hmm),
Without my Uncle Rat's consent (mm-hmm, mm-hmm),
Without my Uncle Rat's consent,
I would not marry the president (mm-hmm, mm-hmm)!

Uncle Rat laughed till he shook his fat sides (mm-hmm, mm-hmm),
Uncle Rat laughed till he shook his fat sides (mm-hmm, mm-hmm),
Uncle Rat laughed till he shook his fat sides,
To think that his niece would be a bride (mm-hmm, mm-hmm)!

Where shall the wedding supper be? (mm-hmm, mm-hmm),
Where shall the wedding supper be? (mm-hmm, mm-hmm),
Where shall the wedding supper be?
Way down yonder in the hallow tree (mm-hmm, mm-hmm)!

What shall the wedding supper be? (mm-hmm, mm-hmm),
What shall the wedding supper be? (mm-hmm, mm-hmm),
What shall the wedding supper be?
Fried mosquito and a black-eyed pea (mm-hmm, mm-hmm)!

First to come in was a flying moth (mm-hmm, mm-hmm),
First to come in was a flying moth (mm-hmm, mm-hmm),
First to come in was a flying moth,
And she laid out the tablecloth (mm-hmm, mm-hmm)!

Next to come in was a doodley bug (mm-hmm, mm-hmm),
Next to come in was a doodley bug (mm-hmm, mm-hmm),
Next to come in was a doodley bug,
Carrying a water jug (mm-hmm, mm-hmm)!

Next to come in was a bumblebee (mm-hmm, mm-hmm),
Next to come in was a bumblebee (mm-hmm, mm-hmm),
Next to come in was a bumblebee,
Set his fiddle on his knee (mm-hmm, mm-hmm)!

Next to come in was a big fat cow (mm-hmm, mm-hmm),
Next to come in was a big fat cow (mm-hmm, mm-hmm),
Next to come in was a big fat cow,
Tried to dance but she didn't know how (mm-hmm, mm-hmm)!

Next to come in was a pussycat (mm-hmm, mm-hmm),
Next to come in was a pussycat (mm-hmm, mm-hmm),
Next to come in was a pussycat,
He ate up the frog and the mouse and the rat (mm-hmm, mm-hmm)!

Little piece of cornbread lying on the shelf (mm-hmm, mm-hmm),
Little piece of cornbread lying on the shelf (mm-hmm, mm-hmm),
Little piece of cornbread lying on the shelf,
If you want any more you can sing it for yourself (mm-hmm, mm-hmm)!

OH DEAR, WHAT CAN THE MATTER BE!

Oh dear, what can the matter be!
Oh dear, what can the matter be!
Oh dear, what can the matter be!
Johnny's so long at the fair.

He promised to bring me a bunch of blue ribbons,
He promised to bring me a bunch of blue ribbons,
He promised to bring me a bunch of blue ribbons,
To tie up my bonny brown hair.

YANKEE DOODLE

Yankee Doodle went to town,
*   riding on a pony,*
Stuck a feather in his cap,
*   and called it macaroni!*

Yankee Doodle, keep it up,
*   Yankee Doodle dandy,*
Mind the music and the step,
*   and with the girls be handy.*

Father and I went down to camp,
*   along with Captain Goodwin,*
And there we saw the men and boys,
*   as thick as hasty puddin'.*

Yankee Doodle, keep it up,
*   Yankee Doodle dandy,*
Mind the music and the step,
*   and with the girls be handy.*

And there was General Washington,
*   Upon a slapping stallion,*
Giving orders to his men,
*   I guess there was a million.*

Yankee Doodle, keep it up,
*   Yankee Doodle dandy,*
Mind the music and the step,
*   and with the girls be handy.*

SHE'LL BE COMING ROUND THE MOUNTAIN

She'll be coming round the mountain
  when she comes (Toot, toot!)
She'll be coming round the mountain
  when she comes (Toot, toot!)
She'll be coming round the mountain,
She'll be coming round the mountain,
She'll be coming round the mountain
  when she comes! (Toot, toot!)

She'll be driving six white horses
  when she comes (Whoa, back!)
She'll be driving six white horses
  when she comes (Whoa, back!)
She'll be driving six white horses,
She'll be driving six white horses,
She'll be driving six white horses
  when she comes! (Whoa, back!)

Oh, we'll all go out to meet her
  when she comes (Howdy do!)
Oh, we'll all go out to meet her
  when she comes (Howdy do!)
Oh, we'll all go out to meet her,
Oh, we'll all go out to meet her,
Oh, we'll all go out to meet her
  when she comes! (Howdy do!)

POLLY, PUT THE KETTLE ON

Polly, put the kettle on,
Polly, put the kettle on,
Polly, put the kettle on,
And we'll all have tea.

Sukey, take it off again,
Sukey, take it off again,
Sukey, take it off again,
They've all gone away.

OVER IN A MEADOW

Over in a meadow, in the sand, in the sun,
Lived an old mother frog and her little froggie one.
"Croak!" said the mother; "I croak," said the one,
So they croaked and they were glad in the sand, in the sun.

Over in a meadow, in a stream so blue,
Lived an old mother fish and her little fishies two.
"Swim!" said the mother; "We swim," said the two,
So they swam and were glad in the stream so blue.

Over in a meadow, in a nest in a tree,
Lived an old mother bird and her little birdies three,
"Tweet!" said the mother; "We tweet," said the three,
So they tweeted and were glad in a nest in a tree.

THE MUFFIN MAN

Oh, do you know the muffin man, the muffin man,
the muffin man,
Oh, do you know the muffin man who lives in
Drury Lane?
Oh, yes, we know the muffin man, the muffin man,
the muffin man,
Oh, yes, we know the muffin man who lives in
Drury Lane.

DO YOUR EARS HANG LOW?

Do your ears hang low?
Do they wobble to and fro?
Can you tie them in a knot?
Can you tie them in a bow?
Can you fling them over your shoulder
Like a Continental soldier?
Do your ears hang low?

(Sung to the tune of "Turkey in the Straw")

When to Start Music Lessons

To instill a passion for musical instruments it is vital that you expose your children to high-quality recordings and live performances (especially yours, if you play) at an early age. Current researchers have concluded that the earlier and more intense the exposure, the more likely it is that your child will take up an instrument of his own or develop his own voice.

Not surprisingly the operative word here is *fun.*

Try taking your child to concerts. Even if he falls asleep, it is fun and helps the child to link cause (instruments and musicians) to effect (exquisite music). It also develops his listening skills even if he doesn't understand specifically what is going on. Home concerts, if you play the piano or another instrument, are particularly effective for establishing music as a means of communication. Your expressions and the range and tempo of the music will affect him deeply. Motion songs (see Chapter Five) and rhythm games are also excellent, because they help to develop a sense of rhythm and, for the child, tie the physical to the musical.

The current raging debate centers on exactly when to start music lessons. One camp, most notably represented by Shinichi Suzuki and his Suzuki Method, starts children as young as two and a half years old on scaled-down instruments, which are often tiny violins. Suzuki advances the notion that musical ability can be taught to a child before he can read notes, just as he learns to speak before he can read. In this case, early instruction is the cornerstone of his philosophy, and hundreds of thousands of children have learned through his method.

Other teachers believe that early instruction leads to discipline problems and ends up being a discouraging experience for parents and child alike. Proponents of a later start usually recommend children wait until the age of seven or even eight before they tackle an instrument. In the early years they suggest that parents introduce primitive instruments like bells and blocks and strongly urge parents to sing motion songs with their children.

While the music theorists thrash it out, parents are best-advised to pin their decision on the mind frame of the individual child. If at three years your child is focused enough to play an instrument, then by all means pursue it. If your nine-year-old is giving you constant grief and resistance about starting up clarinet lessons, don't start. Those who decide to wait on lessons should make sure that the child is impressed with the seriousness of his commitment and is aware of the need for practice. Make an oral contract with him and be sure he is involved in the decision. Once he starts lessons, be his most devoted audience. If he starts wavering, gently direct him back to his commitment. It is important to realize that most children are not reluctant to practice because they find the instrument dreadful but because they find giving up baseball time or television time or playing time dreadful. This is something you can overcome by scheduling his time creatively and by lending him, always and with generosity, your ear.

OLD MACDONALD HAD A FARM

Old MacDonald had a farm,
  Ee-igh, ee-igh, oh!
And on this farm he had some chicks,
  Ee-igh, ee-igh, oh!
With a chick, chick here
  and a chick, chick there,
Here a chick, there a chick,
  everywhere a chick, chick.
Old MacDonald had a farm,
  Ee-igh, ee-igh, oh!

Old MacDonald had a farm,
  Ee-igh, ee-igh, oh!
And on this farm he had some ducks,
  Ee-igh, ee-igh, oh!
With a quack, quack here
  and a quack, quack there,
Here a quack, there a quack,
  everywhere a quack, quack.
With a chick, chick here,
  and a chick, chick there,
Here a chick, there a chick,
  everywhere a chick, chick,
Old MacDonald had a farm,
  Ee-igh, ee-igh, oh!

Old MacDonald had a farm,
  Ee-igh, ee-igh, oh!
And on this farm he had some cows,
  Ee-igh, ee-igh, oh!
With a moo, moo here
  and a moo, moo there,
Here a moo, there a moo,
  everywhere a moo, moo.
With a chick, chick here
  and a chick, chick there,
Here a chick, there a chick,
  everywhere a chick, chick.

With a quack, quack here
  and a quack, quack there,
Here a quack, there a quack,
  everywhere a quack, quack.
Old MacDonald had a farm,
  Ee-igh, ee-igh, oh!

Old MacDonald had a farm,
  Ee-igh, ee-igh, oh!
And on this farm he had some pigs,
  Ee-igh, ee-igh, oh!
With an oink, oink here
  and an oink, oink there,
Here an oink, there an oink,
  everywhere an oink, oink.
With a chick, chick here
  and a chick, chick there,
Here a chick, there a chick,
  everywhere a chick, chick.
With a quack, quack here
  and a quack, quack there,
Here a quack, there a quack,
  everywhere a quack, quack.
With a moo, moo here
  and a moo, moo there,
Here a moo, there a moo,
  everywhere a moo, moo.
Old MacDonald had a farm,
  Ee-igh, ee-igh, oh!

(Add your own animals and verses to Old MacDonald's barnyard.)

OH, SUSANNA!

Oh, I come from Alabama
  with my banjo on my knee,
And I'm going to Louisiana,
  my true love for to see.
It rained all day the day I left,
  The weather it was dry,
The sun so hot, I froze to death,
  Susanna, don't you cry.
Oh, Susanna!
  Oh, don't you cry for me,
I come from Alabama
  with my banjo on my knee.

THE BEAR WENT OVER THE MOUNTAIN

The bear went over the mountain,
The bear went over the mountain,
The bear went over the mountain,
To see what he could see.
And all that he could see,
And all that he could see,
Was the other side of the mountain,
The other side of the mountain,
The other side of the mountain,
Was all that he could see.

IT'S RAINING, IT'S POURING

It's raining, it's pouring,
The old man is snoring,
He went to bed with a hole in his head
And he couldn't get up in the morning.

151

THREE BLIND MICE

Three blind mice,
Three blind mice,
See how they run!
See how they run!
They all ran after the farmer's wife,
Who cut off their tails with the carving knife,
Did you ever hear such a thing in your life,
As three blind mice?

MARY HAD
A LITTLE LAMB

Mary had a little lamb,
  Little lamb, little lamb,
Mary had a little lamb,
  Its fleece was white as snow.

And everywhere that Mary went,
  Mary went, Mary went,
And everywhere that Mary went,
  The lamb was sure to go.

It followed her to school one day,
  To school one day, to school one day,
It followed her to school one day,
  Which was against the rule.

It made the children laugh and play,
  Laugh and play, laugh and play,
It made the children laugh and play,
  To see a lamb in school.

And so the teacher turned him out,
  Turned him out, turned him out,
And so the teacher turned him out,
  But still he lingered near.

JACK AND JILL

Jack and Jill went up the hill
To fetch a pail of water.
Jack fell down and broke his crown
And Jill came tumbling after.

Up Jack got and home did trot
As fast as he could caper.
Went to bed to mend his head
With vinegar and brown paper.

Jill came in and she did grin
To see his paper plaster.
Mother, vexed, did whip her next
For causing Jack's disaster.

OH WHERE, OH WHERE HAS MY LITTLE DOG GONE?

Oh where, oh where has my little dog gone?
Oh where, oh where can he be?
With his ears cut short and his tail cut long,
Oh where, oh where can he be?

ROW, ROW, ROW YOUR BOAT

Row, row, row your boat
Gently down the stream,
Merrily, merrily, merrily, merrily,
Life is but a dream.

BAA BAA BLACK SHEEP

Baa baa black sheep, have you any wool?
Yes sir, yes sir, three bags full,
One for my master and one for my dame,
And one for the little boy that lives in the lane.

Instruments You Can Buy

You can use simple, commercially made instruments to play all kinds of rhythm games with your child. Set your favorite nursery rhymes to music, or ask your child to accompany you as you sing "Yankee Doodle," or "I've Been Working on the Railroad," or any of your personal favorites.

Children love **jingle clogs,** colorful sticks with metal discs attached on either side that make a pretty sound when you shake them. **Cymbals** come in a variety of sizes, and **tambourines** are always fun. Around his second birthday he'll be ready to twang a **triangle,** but watch out for the "twanger"; it must not be poked in anyone's mouth or eyes. A word of caution about **slide whistles,** too. They make a nice sound but should not be used when the child is running around. As your child approaches age three, you might want to invest in some **bell blocks** and **resonator bells.** These are usually fixed on a frame like a **xylophone** and can be struck with a small mallet or drumstick. **Rhythm sticks** can be purchased notched or plain and in many colors. They are used in pairs to beat rhythm. **Claves** are metal cylinders on a stick that click when you shake them. Wooden **tone blocks** also make a clicky sound when you hit them with a stick. **Maracas** are oval-shaped objects with beans inside, also on a stick. Having one to shake in each hand puts anyone in a festive mood.

Department stores with good toy sections usually carry most of these musical instruments. Shops that specialize in musical instruments will have more. If there is an educational supplies store near you, you should be able to find what you want. Or write to Music in Motion for their catalog at: 109 Spanish Village, Suite 645, Dallas, Texas 75248. You can call toll free 1-800-445-0649. They sell everything related to teaching and having fun with music.

Classical Music

All classical music that is bright and varied is good for children. I cannot, for example, imagine almost anything written by Bach that would not appeal on some level to a child. True, dour organ music and modern opera might not be as captivating as *Peter and the Wolf*, but this, I presume, goes without saying. There are some pieces, however, that were written especially with children in mind, and my favorites follow. Enjoy.

Debussy, Claude. Piano music from *The Children's Corner Suite*. This suite, in six parts, was composed for children by Debussy and dedicated to his daughter. "Serenade for the Doll" is a particularly appealing piece. Some others are entitled "Golliwog's Cakewalk," "Snow Is Dancing," and "The Little Shepherd."

Dukas, Paul. Children love to hear the music based on Goethe's cautionary tale of *The Sorcerer's Apprentice,* about a young lad who gets hold of the sorcerer's book of magic and starts to make magic spells he can't stop.

Mussorgsky, Modest. *Pictures at an Exhibition* was originally written for piano, then rescored for orchestra by Maurice Ravel. Many parts of it, such as "The Gnome," "The Old Castle," and "The Hut of Baba-Yaga" evoke visual images that are very appealing to children.

Prokofiev, Sergey. Children who know the story of "Cinderella" will appreciate the lyrical romance of Prokofiev's musical version of the tale.

Ravel, Maurice. In the *Mother Goose Suite* Ravel tells more familiar tales in music, including "Sleeping Beauty," "Hop o' My Thumb," "Little Ugly One," and "Conversations of Beauty and the Beast."

Rimsky-Korsakov, Nikolay. Young or old, who could fail to respond to the excitement of *Scheherazade?*

Rossini, Gioacchino. The album entitled *The William Tell Overture* with Eugene Ormandy conducting the Philadelphia Orchestra includes that classic and many other pieces suitable for listening with children.

Saint-Saëns, C. *Carnival of the Animals* is a collection of short pieces that suggest different animals: the lion, chicken, swan, turtle, kangaroo. (Ogden Nash has written verses to accompany each one.)

Poulenc, Francis. Peter Ustinov tells the story of Babar the Elephant by Jean de Brunhoff, as well as "The Little Tailor" by the Brothers Grimm with music by Tibor Harsanyi on a record put out by Angel.

The album entitled *Bernstein Conducts for Young People* (New York Philharmonic) includes many old favorites mentioned above, plus *Peter and the Wolf* by Prokofiev, *Till Eulenspiegel's Merry Pranks* by Richard Strauss, and *Danse Macabre* by Saint-Saëns. Most narrations are by Leonard Bernstein.

Best Kids' Records

Here is my personal listing of the best, most enticing, and original children's records and tapes. My suggestion is to select a few of the following records and to test them out with your child. Since they are rather expensive, you might want to check some out at your local library, which most likely has a listening room and a lenders' collection.

If your child doesn't take to a particular album, try it again the next day or the next week. He will get hooked. And once he gets hooked, he will want to hear it over and over again. However, don't limit his listening to children's music.

I tend to agree with current wisdom that argues against an *overload* of children's music at the expense of the other many and diverse kinds of music. Children can understand and appreciate jazz, show tunes, classical —any kind of music you choose. So proceed with a sense of moderation. The more diversity you give your child, the more musically developed he will become.

A–Z Animal Alphabet Songs. Can you name an animal for each letter of the alphabet? The members of this musical menagerie can, with whimsical rhymes about creatures from alligators to zebras. The musical background ranges from classical to jazz rock.

The Baby Record. Sesame Street's Bob McGrath and music educator Katharine Smithrim lead parents in singing and acting out songs with baby. Side one is best for infants; side two is for toddlers. *Songs and Games for Toddlers* introduces more rhymes, songs, and games for two- and three-year-olds.

The Baby Sitters. An unconventional collection of old and new songs recorded by Alan Arkin in his living room with family and friends.

Baby Song. Hap and Martha Palmer play jazz and simple rock and roll to accompany the everyday activities of the very young child. The older child will enjoy *Learning Basic Skills Through Music* and *Getting to Know Myself.*

Big Bird Leads the Band. Big Bird teaches music appreciation to young children with the orchestra playing old favorites ("Frère Jacques," "Twinkle, Twinkle, Little Star") and variations on old favorites ("The Mary Had a Little Lamb March"). *Discover the Orchestra* is equally informative and amusing at the same time.

Birds, Beasts, Bugs and Little Fishes and *Birds, Beasts, Bugs and Bigger Fishes.* Pete Seeger sings all about animals. Both albums include his renditions of traditional favorites such as "Foolish Frog" and "Old Paint." More Pete Seeger titles to collect and enjoy as children grow older: *Folk Songs for Young People* and *American Folk Songs.*

The Cat Came Back. Anyone who ever heard the title song from this album by Fred Penner will find himself trying to remember all the words at the most unlikely times. Equally appealing are the songs and lyrics from *The Polka Dot Pony* and *Special Delivery.*

Counting Games and Rhythms for the Little Ones. Ella Jenkins leads listeners in counting, skipping, chanting, and hopping to "One, Two, Buckle My Shoe" and other songs, rhythms, and rhymes in this album. *Play Your Instruments and Make a Pretty Sound* offers songs for the preschooler, performed by Jenkins with a children's rhythm band.

Dance, Sing and Learn. Be a seed or a sail or a train with Esther Nelson. Electronic jazz piano and steel drums are just part of the musical accompaniment to which youngsters move, dance, and stretch their imaginations.

Golden Slumbers. Pete Seeger and others sing popular lullabies from near and far.

In Harmony II. On this Grammy Award–winning disc and its predecessor, *In Harmony I,* we hear Bruce Springsteen, Linda Ronstadt, and Bette Midler, as well as Ernie and the Cookie Monster from Sesame Street singing songs you may have heard before—but not like this!

Little White Duck and Other Children's Favorites. Accompanied by guitar, Burl Ives sings "The Little Engine that Could," "Mr. Froggie Went a-Courtin'," and many others.

Lullabies for Little Dreamers. The dulcimer and other instruments provide the background for Brahms's "Lullaby," "Over the Rainbow," and other songs to lull little ones to sleep.

Mister Rogers. His records and cassettes offer his own special brand of whimsy and chat about all things that concern children. Look for *You Are Special, A Place of Our Own, Won't You Be My Neighbor?,* and *Let's Be Together Today.*

Music for Ones and Twos and *More Music for Ones and Twos.* Tom Glazer encourages little folks to listen and observe as he plays and sings.

On the Move with Greg and Steve. This album and others in the Younghearts Series teach rhythm and movement. *Quiet Moment* suggests quiet activities and offers good music for resting.

Peter, Paul and Mommy. Peter, Paul and Mary bring back the sixties with "Puff, the Magic Dragon" and add many more songs about fanciful animals. On the flip side are great tunes about toys.

Raffi. My favorite. This popular French Canadian has a series of records starting with *Singable Songs for the Very Young.* Others in the series are *More Singable Songs, The Corner Grocery Store, Baby Beluga,* and *One Light, One Sun.*

Rosenshontz Tickles You. Clown around with Gary Rosen on the guitar and Bill Shontz playing almost any instrument you can name. You'll hear old favorites like "The Teddy Bears' Picnic" and new ones including "Sam, the Tickle Man" and "Hippopotamus Rock." *Share It* and *It's the Truth* are two more popular albums by this pair.

Sharon, Lois and Bram. This trio from Canada will have you grinning and tapping your foot right along with your little one. *Mainly Mother Goose* is an ingeniously funny addition to their ongoing series. *One Elephant, Deux Elephants* and *Smorgasbord* are equally innovative and amusing to young and old.

Wee Sing Nursery Rhymes and Lullabies. Favorite rhymes, simple melodies, distinct rhythm patterns make this an excellent tape for early listening. It is a good choice for quiet times, too, or to keep baby amused during a long car ride.

CHAPTER FIVE

Motion Songs and Finger Plays

"O body swayed to music, O brightening glance,
How can we know the dancer from the dance?"
—William Butler Yeats,
"Among School Children"

INTRODUCTION

In the early years children divide up their time between two very fundamental objectives: movement and speech. These skills are the stepping-stones to independence, and as parents, we stand expectantly on the sidelines, waiting to cheer "first steps" and "first words."

Our children fight hard for these developmental firsts. In fact, so much concentration is required of them that they generally can focus on only one area at a time, working on movement for a while and, having succeeded, moving on to speech (or vice versa). This is why motion songs and finger plays, which combine the two primary achievements of early childhood, have been recognized as perfect entertainments for the developing child.

Like fairy tales and rhymes and fables, these little songs and rhymes are not new. They are simply more gems from our repository of folk culture, gems that shine brilliantly against the rather dull innovations of our age. A teacher of the nineteenth century invented this one; a mother in England created that one. Children picked them up and would not let them go. And so today, the most gifted librarians, teachers, and parents use them to make merry, to develop coordination and to build language.

For the most part it will be *you* who is the little teapot or the farmer (in the dell) at first. Infants who haven't crossed that "first-word" or "first-step" line cannot be expected to do much more than "Pat-a-Cake." That doesn't mean you should put aside this book until your child is eighteen months old. On the contrary, you ought to start at once because your child will not only find you amusing but also he will get an important familiarity with the material and acquire a sense of rhythm. Try one of the following selections and see if your eight-month-old does not sway with you.

I started Virginia with "This Little Piggy" when she was just two months old, mainly because it was one of the few things I remembered. It helped her become aware of the fact that she has feet, for one thing, but it also provided an excellent source of physical stimulation: she loved to be tickled at the end. At thirteen months she would bob her head up and down to the chant. At seventeen months I emphasized the word *this,* and one by one she would grab my toes—clumsily, to be sure, but nevertheless as an active participant. She now does the finger play with her doll while I chant the rhyme. I look forward to the day when she will be able to form words, but at this point I have succeeded in taking her from a passive stance to an important, engaged level of activity. Making this leap from passive to active is in great measure what the first two years are all about.

The songs and rhymes in this chapter represent an amalgam of actual finger plays ("The Itsy Bitsy Spider") and singing games ("Going Round the Mulberry Bush"). Most of the selections can be played with two people, you and your child, but some of them require four people. If you are always at a loss for a third and fourth person, you can probably amend the action to make it work for two. Whatever the case, be creative with your selections. You can use "Ten Little Indians" to teach your child about numbers or "This Old Man" to teach your child about the parts of the body.

In addition, you should try your hand at inventing motion songs or games on your own. One game I have seen played successfully is to have your child clap hands to music, speeding up for fast movements and slowing down to lazy rhythms. The entire process of "getting the beat" is important, elemental training that you can conduct at home. Let your imagination offer you variations on these whimsical pieces and you will have hours of diversion.

Since many of us have forgotten the classic games of childhood, I decided to collect a few of my favorite (and forgotten) and present them in this section. Most of the games are "games that teach," and they involve the same kind of processes (thought and action) you will find in the motion songs and finger plays. Games are tremendous for building social skills. Introduce them as early as you can. Not only will you help your child to understand that risks are part of life, but also you will help him to build confidence.

Indeed, the more you use the following verses and games to "socialize" with your child, the more prepared he will be for the world outside of your home. Learning how to play is your child's work, and it is not as easy as it appears. Let these songs, rhymes, and games give him a warm and witty hand.

TEN FINGERS

I have ten little fingers
(Follow action as rhyme indicates.)
And they all belong to me.
I can make them do things.
Would you like to see?
I can shut them up tight
Or open them wide.
I can put them together
Or make them all hide.
I can make them jump high,
I can make them jump low,
I can fold them quietly
And hold them just so.

KING OF FRANCE

The famous King of France,
He led ten thousand men.
He marched them way, way up the hill
(March hands up in air, one over other.)
And marched them down again.
(March hands down.)
And when they were up, they were up, up, up
(March hands up.)
And when they were down, they were down, down, down
(March hands down.)
And when they were only halfway up,
(Hold hands halfway up.)
They were neither up nor down.
(Move hands up, then down, very quickly.)

165

GRANDMA'S SPECTACLES

Here are Grandma's spectacles,
   (Make circles with thumbs and index fingers placed over eyes.)
And here is Grandma's hat,
   (Join hands at fingertips and place on top of head.)
And here's the way she folds her hands
   (Fold hands and place gently in lap.)
And puts them in her lap.

Here are Grandpa's spectacles
   (Make larger circles with thumbs and index fingers and place over eyes.)
And here is Grandpa's hat,
   (Make larger pointed hat, as above.)
And here's the way he folds his arms
   (Fold arms with vigor.)
And sits like that.

TEN LITTLE INDIANS

One little, two little, three little Indians;
Four little, five little, six little Indians;
Seven little, eight little, nine little Indians;
Ten little Indian boys.
Show a finger at each count.

PAT-A-CAKE

Pat-a-cake, pat-a-cake, baker's man,
   (Clap hands.)
Bake me a cake as fast as you can,
   (Cup one hand loosely, palm up; rotate finger of other hand in cupped palm.)
Pat it and prick it and mark it with B
   (Pat hands firmly.)
And put it in the oven for baby and me.
   (Move hand forward slowly.)

GOING ROUND THE MULBERRY BUSH

CHORUS:

We all go round the mulberry bush,
the mulberry bush,
the mulberry bush,
We all go round the mulberry bush
so early in the morning.

This is the way we wash our clothes,
we wash our clothes,
we wash our clothes,
This is the way we wash our clothes
All of a Monday morning.

This is the way we iron our clothes,
we iron our clothes,
we iron our clothes,
This is the way we iron our clothes
All of a Tuesday morning.

This is the way we scrub our floor,
we scrub our floor,
we scrub our floor,
This is the way we scrub our floor
All of a Wednesday morning.

This is the way we mend our clothes,
we mend our clothes,
we mend our clothes,
This is the way we mend our clothes
All of a Thursday morning.

This is the way we sweep the house,
we sweep the house,
we sweep the house,
This is the way we sweep the house
All of a Friday morning.

This is the way we bake our bread,
we bake our bread,
we bake our bread,
This is the way we bake our bread
All of a Saturday morning.

This is the way we go to church,
go to church,
go to church,
This is the way we go to church
All of a Sunday morning.

Act out the movements suggested in each verse. For "baking the bread" you can knead the dough. For "going to church" you can make a steeple with your hands over your head and march in place. At the chorus you can all join hands and circle around.

TWO BLACKBIRDS

There were two blackbirds
  (Hold up two fists and wiggle index finger on each hand.)
Sitting on a hill,
  (Lift both hands up to imaginary hill.)
The one named Jack,
  (Wiggle one index finger.)
The other named Jill.
  (Wiggle the other index finger.)
Fly away, Jack!
  (One hand flies away.)
Fly away, Jill!
  (The other hand flies away.)
Come again, Jack!
  (One hand returns.)
Come again, Jill!
  (The other hand returns.)

DID YOU EVER SEE A LASSIE?

Did you ever see a lassie,
  a lassie, a lassie?
Did you ever see a lassie
  go this way and that?
Go this way and that way,
  and this way and that way?
Did you ever see a lassie,
  go this way and that?
Can be repeated replacing *lassie* with *laddie.*

For this you need at least four people, preferably many more. Form a circle and have one person stand in the middle. Join hands and sing, circling to the left. When you get to *go this way and that,* the child in the middle creates an action, like clapping or patting his head, whatever his choosing. All players imitate the actions. At the song's end, the child in the middle chooses another player to be "it."

BLUEBIRD, BLUEBIRD

Bluebird, bluebird, through my window,
Bluebird, bluebird, through my window,
Bluebird, bluebird, through my window
Oh, Johnny, I am tired!

Take a little girl and tap her on the shoulder,
Take a little girl and tap her on the shoulder,
Take a little girl and tap her on the shoulder,
Oh, Johnny, I am tired!

Bluebird, bluebird, through my window,
Bluebird, bluebird, through my window,
Bluebird, bluebird, through my window
Oh, Johnny, I am tired!

This game requires at least eight players to be fun. Everyone joins hands, then lifts them to form archlike shapes. The first player weaves in and out of the arches as the first verse is sung. At the second verse the first player taps a second player on the shoulder. Players one and two are now both bluebirds and weave in and out of the arches. This goes on and on until all players are bluebirds. At the song's end everyone can collapse on the floor at "I am tired!"

I'M A LITTLE TEAPOT

I'm a little teapot, short and stout,
   (Puff yourself up in a standing position.)
Here is my handle, here is my spout.
   (Put your left hand on your waist; cock your right hand and elbow like a spout.)
When I get all steamed up, I will shout,
   (Lean to your left.)
Tip me over and pour me out.
   (Lean to your right to "pour out.")

THIS OLD MAN

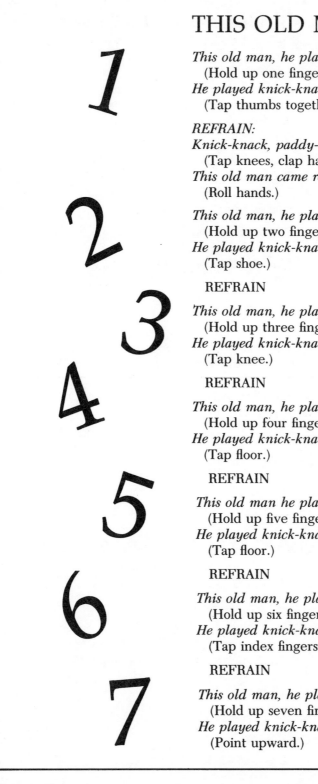

This old man, he played one,
  (Hold up one finger.)
He played knick-knack on his thumb.
  (Tap thumbs together.)

REFRAIN:
Knick-knack, paddy-whack, give a dog a bone,
  (Tap knees, clap hands, extend one hand.)
This old man came rolling home.
  (Roll hands.)

This old man, he played two,
  (Hold up two fingers.)
He played knick-knack on his shoe.
  (Tap shoe.)

REFRAIN

This old man, he played three,
  (Hold up three fingers.)
He played knick-knack on his knee.
  (Tap knee.)

REFRAIN

This old man, he played four,
  (Hold up four fingers.)
He played knick-knack on the floor.
  (Tap floor.)

REFRAIN

This old man he played five,
  (Hold up five fingers.)
He played knick-knack on his drive.
  (Tap floor.)

REFRAIN

This old man, he played six,
  (Hold up six fingers.)
He played knick-knack on his sticks.
  (Tap index fingers.)

REFRAIN

This old man, he played seven,
  (Hold up seven fingers.)
He played knick-knack straight to heaven.
  (Point upward.)

REFRAIN

This old man, he played eight,
  (Hold up eight fingers.)
He played knick-knack on his garden gate.
  (Open and close imaginary gate.)

REFRAIN

This old man, he played nine,
  (Hold up nine fingers.)
He played knick-knack on his spine.
  (Tap spine.)

REFRAIN

This old man, he played ten,
  (Hold up ten fingers.)
He played knick-knack now and then.
  (Clap hands.)

REFRAIN

8

9

10

Motion Songs Build Coordination

Though the ability to synchronize a movement with rhythmic stimuli is not usually developed until a child is about three years old, you can help your child build coordination of sound and movement by improvising actions to accompany the rhymes you say together. The rhymes in this section, accompanied by the appropriate movements, are excellent for starters. As your child grows older he'll want to move on from rhymes to songs with more elaborate movements.

Draw your child's attention to the natural rhythms of everyday movement by making up word rhymes to go with walking, skipping, and running. For example:

Sometimes I walk, slowly, slowly, slowly,
Other times I hurry, hurry, hurry,
Often I skip for fun, for fun, for fun,
But when I want to get there fast,
I run, run, run.

You can accompany these word rhythms and movements with the sound of hand clapping, drumbeats, or a tambourine. Vary the basic movements to create new ones and accompany songs in this book, as well as folk songs and other music your child hears on records, tapes, and discs. Show him how to move to the rhythm of a Strauss waltz. Watch how he moves when he hears rock and roll. Talk about why such movements are different.

As a result of such simple exercises, you'll notice a marked increase in his ability to coordinate movement to sound.

PAWPAW PATCH

Where, oh where is pretty little Sally?
Where, oh where is pretty little Sally?
Where, oh where is pretty little Sally?
Way down yonder in the pawpaw patch.

Come on, boys, let's go find her,
Come on, boys, let's go find her,
Come on, boys, let's go find her,
Way down yonder in the pawpaw patch.

Picking up pawpaws, put 'em in your
pocket,
Picking up pawpaws, put 'em in your
pocket,
Picking up pawpaws, put 'em in your
pocket,
Way down yonder in the pawpaw patch.

Hold her tight so you won't lose her,
Hold her tight so you won't lose her,
Hold her tight so you won't lose her,
Way down yonder in the pawpaw patch.

Pick a player to be "it." Use his first name in the first verse (for a boy, say "Where, oh where is *our* little Tommy"). Everyone stands in a circle singing the first verse with their eyes covered. "It," meanwhile, runs and hides. At the second verse everyone opens their eyes and sings, skipping about and looking for "it." They keep singing the second verse until "it" is found. Once he is found, everyone sings the third verse, acting out the words from wherever they are standing. At the fourth verse everyone circles around "it," holds hands, and skips back to the original starting place with "it" in the middle.

GO ROUND AND ROUND THE VILLAGE

Go round and round the village,
Go round and round the village,
Go round and round the village,
As we have done before.

Go in and out the window,
Go in and out the window,
Go in and out the window,
As we have done before.

Follow me to London,
Follow me to London,
Follow me to London,
As we have done before.

Stand and face your partner,
Stand and face your partner,
Stand and face your partner,
As we have done before.

Now shake his hand and leave him,
Now shake his hand and leave him,
Now shake his hand and leave him,
As we have done before.

Children form a circle and "it" stands in the middle. First verse, he runs around the circle as everyone sings. Second verse, all the children join hands and lift them to form arches. "It" goes in and out of the arches. Third verse, "it" picks a partner and they both go in and out of the arches. Fourth verse, the two go to the middle of the circle and stand and bow to each other, with each line (three bows in all). The fifth verse, they shake hands and "it" returns to the circle while the second player prepares to become the new "it." Repeat until everyone has a chance to be "it."

LOOBY LOO

Here we go looby loo,
Here we go looby light,
Here we go looby loo,
All on a Saturday night.

I put my right hand in,
I take my right hand out,
I give my right hand a shake, shake, shake,
And turn myself about.

Here we go looby loo,
Here we go looby light,
Here we go looby loo,
All on a Saturday night.

I put my left hand in,
I take my left hand out,
I give my left hand a shake, shake, shake,
And turn myself about.

Here we go looby loo,
Here we go looby light,
Here we go looby loo,
All on a Saturday night.

I put my right foot in,
I take my right foot out,
I give my right foot a shake, shake, shake,
And turn myself about.

Here we go looby loo,
Here we go looby light,
Here we go looby loo,
All on a Saturday night.

I put my left foot in,
I take my left foot out,
I give my left foot a shake, shake, shake,
And turn myself about.

Here we go looby loo,
Here we go looby light,
Here we go looby loo,
All on a Saturday night.

I put my whole self in,
I take my whole self out,
I give my whole self a shake, shake, shake,
And turn myself about.

Any number can play this. Form a circle, and for the chorus walk to the circle's center and then back, with the music. For every other verse simply follow the instructions in place.

LONDON BRIDGE

London Bridge is falling down,
Falling down, falling down.
London Bridge is falling down,
My Fair Lady.

Build it up with iron bars,
Iron bars, iron bars,
Build it up with iron bars,
My Fair Lady.

Iron bars will rust away,
Rust away, rust away,
Iron bars will rust away,
My Fair Lady.

Build it up with pins and needles,
Pins and needles, pins and needles,
Build it up with pins and needles,
My Fair Lady.

Here's a prisoner I have got,
I have got, I have got,
Here's a prisoner I have got,
My Fair Lady.

Take the key and lock him up,
Lock him up, lock him up,
Take the key and lock him up,
My Fair Lady.

Two children join hands and lift them to form arches. They privately decide which is "silver" and which is "gold." As the song begins, the remaining children form a single line and skip through the arches. When they get to "My Fair Lady," the arches capture whomever is between them. The captured child is given the choice: "What will you pay? Silver or gold?" He chooses one and then lines up behind who ever he picked. This goes on and on until the two "teams" have formed, and then, as is the custom, a tug of war is held between the two.

WHERE IS THUMBKIN?

Where is thumbkin, where is thumbkin?
  (Put your hands behind your back.)
Here I am, here I am.
  (One thumb comes out and is bent up
and down to the music. Then the other comes out.)
How are you today, sir?
  (First thumb bends up and down.)
Very well, I thank you,
  (Second thumb bends up and down.)
Run away, run away.
  (Thumb flies away; other thumb flies away.)

Where is pointer, where is pointer?
  (Repeat above with first finger.)
Here I am, here I am.
How are you today, sir?
Very well, I thank you,
Run away, run away.

Where is tall man, where is tall man?
  (Repeat above with middle finger.)
Here I am, here I am.
How are you today, sir?
Very well, I thank you,
Run away, run away.

Where is ring man, where is ring man?
  (Repeat above with ring finger.)
Here I am, here I am.
How are you today, sir?
Very well, I thank you,
Run away, run away.

Where is pinkie, where is pinkie?
  (Repeat above with little finger.)
Here I am, here I am.
How are you today, sir?
Very well, I thank you,
Run away, run away.

Where are all the men, where are all the men?
  (Repeat above with whole hand.)
Here we are, here we are.
How are you today, sirs?
Very well, we thank you,
Run away, run away.

A TISKET, A TASKET

A tisket, a tasket,
A green and yellow basket.
I wrote a letter to my love,
And on the way I dropped it.
I dropped it, I dropped it,
And on the way I dropped it.
A little boy (girl) picked it up,
And put it in his (her) pocket.

Children join hands and form a circle. Player is named "it." "It" takes a handkerchief and starts skipping around the circle. At "I dropped it" he drops the handkerchief and continues (now running) in the same direction. The player behind whom he dropped the handkerchief takes off in the opposite direction, and the two race for the empty spot. The loser takes the handkerchief for the next round.

Mr. Crabbie's Garden

This is a fun game that employs music, coordination, and the imagination. It's called Mr. Crabbie's Garden, for no apparent reason, but the "garden," as it were, can be your living room or your backyard or any relatively open space. Gather a good number of children—at least six for a good game. Appoint one player to be "it" or Mr. Crabbie. Mr. Crabbie turns on a record. At that moment everyone runs around wildly, acting like their favorite animal (elephant, horse, lizard, whatever).

Mr. Crabbie suddenly stops the music after a good bit of romping has taken place, and at that moment all of the animals fall down where they are, playacting "dead" with their eyes closed. Mr. Crabbie comes out, bellowing, "Let me see if I can find any animals in my garden." He walks up to each animal, one at a time, and tests for "limpness" by lifting up an arm or a leg, which—if the child is relaxed—should fall easily to the floor. If the child is stiff, he is caught and is sent "off to the forest"—i.e., out of the game. If he is relaxed, Mr. Crabbie simply moves on. The game starts again and is played until all of the children are out.

RING AROUND A ROSY

Ring around a rosy,
A pocket full of posies.
Ashes, ashes,
We all fall down.

Join hands and form a circle. Skip to the left until
"we all fall down" and then (gently) all fall down.

THE ITSY BITSY SPIDER

Oh, the itsy, bitsy spider went up the water spout,
   (Put opposite thumb to forefinger on both hands and
alternate connecting each to each in an upward motion.)
Down came the rain and washed the spider out,
   (Both hands shake downward and push out.)
Out came the sun and dried up all the rain,
   (Join hands above head to imitate sun.)
And the itsy, bitsy spider went up the spout again.
   (Connect opposite thumbs and forefingers again and repeat
upward motion.)

HERE IS THE CHURCH

Here is the church,
   (Join hands and interlock fingers, with fingers down
and knuckles showing.)
And here is the steeple.
   (Lift two forefingers to form a steeple.)
Open the doors,
   (Interlock all fingers, including forefingers again,
and turn palms upward.)
And see all the people.
   (Wiggle all fingers.)

BINGO

There was a farmer had a dog,
And Bingo was his name, oh.
B-I-N-G-O, B-I-N-G-O, B-I-N-G-O,
And Bingo was his name, oh!

Sing through once, slowly. Sing again, a little faster and substitute a clap for the *B*. Repeat, even faster, and substitute two claps, one for the *B* and one for the *I*. Repeat until *Bingo* has been replaced completely by claps.

OATS, PEAS, BEANS

Oats, peas, beans, and barley grow,
Oats, peas, beans, and barley grow,
Do you, or I, or anyone know,
How oats, peas, beans, and barley grow?

First the farmer sows his seed,
Then he stands and takes his ease,
He stamps his foot and claps his hands,
And turns around to view his lands.

Waiting for a partner,
Waiting for a partner,
Open the ring and take her in,
While we gaily dance and sing.

A player is picked to be "it"; he is the farmer. All children join hands and form a circle around the farmer and, in the first verse, skip to the left. Second verse: Farmer acts out each line, sowing the seed, surveying the land, stamping, clapping, and turning around. Third verse: The farmer selects a partner, pulls her into the middle, and all skip around them. The partner becomes the new farmer.

THE FARMER IN THE DELL

The farmer in the dell,
The farmer in the dell,
Heigh-ho, the derry oh,
The farmer in the dell.

The farmer takes a wife,
The farmer takes a wife,
Heigh-ho, the derry oh,
The farmer takes a wife.

The wife takes a nurse,
The wife takes a nurse,
Heigh-ho, the derry oh,
The wife takes a nurse.

The nurse takes a child,
The nurse takes a child,
Heigh-ho, the derry oh,
The nurse takes a child.

The child takes a dog,
The child takes a dog,
Heigh-ho, the derry oh,
The child takes a dog.

The dog takes a cat,
The dog takes a cat,
Heigh-ho, the derry-oh,
The dog takes a cat.

The cat takes a rat,
The cat takes a rat,
Heigh-ho, the derry-oh,
The cat takes a rat.

The rat takes the cheese,
The rat takes the cheese,
Heigh-ho, the derry-oh,
The rat takes the cheese.

The cheese stands alone,
The cheese stands alone,
Heigh-ho, the derry-oh,
The cheese stands alone.

Here, again, you'll need a lot of children to make it a fun motion song. All form a circle. "It" is in the middle; he is the "farmer." Children circle to the left while they sing the first verse. "It" chooses a wife, the wife chooses a nurse, and so on, until all of the children are in the middle. When there is only one left, sing the "cheese stands alone" verse.

THIS LITTLE PIGGY

This little piggy went to market,
This little piggy stayed home,
This little piggy had roast beef,
This little piggy had none,
And this little piggy cried,
   Wee-wee, wee-wee,
All the way home.

Pull your child's foot up into a comfortable position. Start with the big toe, pinching it gently with line one. Move on down through all of the toes, line by line, until you get to the little piggy who cries "wee-wee" and race your hands up the child's leg to tickle him.

Musical Chairs

I don't think one can actually go through an American childhood without playing musical chairs. It would be a true deprivation, like not ever having played Pin the Tail on the Donkey or never having taken a cakewalk. But in case you forgot this little American classic, here it is.

First, assemble as many children as you can. There is absolutely no limit on how many can play. You will need a record player, and someone to monitor it. You will also need to line up some chairs in a row (or in a circle facing out), depending on how many players you have. *Start out with one less chair than you have players.* Have the "music monitor" start the music. When the music starts, everyone begins to walk around the chairs in an orderly progression and to the beat of the music. The music monitor will arbitrarily stop the music, and at that point everyone grabs a chair and sits down. The person who is left without a chair is out. Repeat the whole process now, removing one chair after each round. Play until there are only two players left and one chair. After they battle it out, the game is over.

CHAPTER SIX

Lullabies

"Music that gentlier on the spirit lies,
Than tired eyelids on tired eyes."
—Alfred, Lord Tennyson

INTRODUCTION

The most astonishing example of "lulling" I have seen did not happen in a child's nursery or in the arms of a fine Austrian nanny but in the supermodern Narita International Airport. There, after what seemed an endless flight from Los Angeles, my sister and I braced ourselves for the dreaded cattle drive of testy passengers, lost luggage, and the menacing phalanx of unpredictable customs officials.

Instead we were greeted by Bach.

There were more than three hundred of us, all cranky, all Americans, and all bedazzled by the musical spell. One by one, as we entered the gate, we became uncommonly quiet, and if we spoke at all, we did so in hushed, almost reverential voices. My sister thought we had been rerouted to Notre Dame. I was astounded. A simple song had soothed us all and had done so in an instant.

The reason I mention this is because I truly believe that the average day takes its toll upon a child in a manner most resembling an international flight. Kids seem to have jet lag every day; they get tired and wired and restless and exhausted. Like no other medium, a lullaby can cast a child off to exactly where he wants to be, which is asleep. The following collection of children's lullabies have escorted millions of children to never-never land, and I think you will love them.

You can start singing lullabies to your child before he is born; at twelve weeks the fetus can hear your voice quite clearly. Recent research suggests that babies have an uncanny recognition of those songs they heard while in the womb. We also know that pregnant women benefit tremendously from relaxation and that soothing music helps immensely. There is no such thing as starting too soon.

As the parent of a newborn, you will find that lullabies are as much a part of the nighttime feeding as milk and rocking chairs. I remember marveling at how big and clumsy my voice seemed compared to my little girls in the first days of their lives. I was almost afraid to sing to them, so I hummed softly at first. After a while (and to the chagrin of my husband) I lost my inhibitions. I started singing up a storm, and I don't know that I've ever stopped.

Powerful nighttime rituals are the result of two things: absolute consistency and absolute flexibility. On the one hand, you should find a song or two that your child likes and stick to it. On the other hand, you must be aware of the need for change and be sensitive enough to change your songs or quit singing completely, if only for a while.

For instance, my older daughter relied on a nighttime bottle until she was about thirteen months old. Up to that point I used to sing to her and let her sip her way into slumber. Once she was weened, she spent about four months just "passing out" at night, and I didn't sing to her at all for fear of arousing her. Now she almost requires a show worthy of Busby Berkley to get her to sleep. I generally tell her a story in her room or in the dimly lit living room, sing to her for a while, and end with a prayer. In a few months our ritual will probably change.

A caution: Children have a very different sense of reality, and they can easily come to regard a song as tangible and as comforting as their love blanket or a cherished doll. If your child needs to hear "All Through the Night" or a beloved story before bed, be certain to let your baby-sitter know it. You will avert a lot of tears and confusion.

Finally, while lullabies are important for children, they can also be revitalizing for adults. When you sing to your child, let a peace surround the two of you. If you decide to let the day slip off your shoulders, the anxiety will also slip from your child. A favorite verse of mine comes to mind:

> And the night shall be filled with music,
> And the cares that infest the day,
> Shall fold their tents like the Arabs,
> And as silently steal away.*

Good night.

---

* "The Day Is Done" by Henry Wadsworth Longfellow, 1845.

ALL THE PRETTY
LITTLE HORSES

Hush-a-bye, don't you cry,
Go to sleep, little baby;
When you wake, you shall have cake,
And all the pretty little horses.
Black and bay, dapple and gray,
Coach and six white horses,
All the pretty little horses.

ALL THROUGH
THE NIGHT

Sleep, my child, and peace attend thee,
All through the night;
Guardian angels God will send thee,
All through the night;
Soft and drowsy hours are creeping,
Hill and vale in slumber sleeping,
I my loving vigil keeping,
All through the night.

While the moon her watch is keeping,
All through the night;
While the weary world is sleeping,
All through the night.
O'er thy spirit gently stealing,
Visions of delight revealing,
Breathes a pure and holy feeling,
All through the night.

AU CLAIR DE LA LUNE
(BY THE LIGHT
OF THE MOONSHINE)

Au clair de la lune,
  Mon ami Pierrot,
Prête-moi ta plume
  Pour écrire un mot.
Ma chandelle est morte,
  Je n'ai plus de feu;
Prête-moi ta plume
  Pour l'amour de Dieu.

ENGLISH TRANSLATION

By the light of moonshine,
  My good friend Pierrot,
Lend to me your pen,
  So I may write a note.
See, my candle's guttered,
  Dim and chill my way;
Lend it to me,
  For the love of God, I pray.

BYE, BABY BUNTING

Bye, baby bunting,
Daddy's gone a-hunting,
To get a little rabbit skin
To wrap his baby bunting in.

How to Lullaby

Lullabies are different from other songs because they carry the specific burden of easing your child to rest. It takes a light touch and patience, but once you master the art of lullabying, it will add extraordinary pleasure to your evening. Here are a few thoughts to consider:

- *Watch your child's reaction.* Infants are often more responsive to certain tempos and pitch ranges than to others. If the child seems restless or irritated, try something else—a different pace, a different volume, maybe even another song. Many infants have highly developed preferences.

- *Be aware of your child's mood.* A gentle lullaby is not suitable for a child who is still keyed up and rearing to go. Try something lively at first, then begin to calm him down with a more soothing tone at a slower tempo. If you are arousing your child, you might start off with a slow, melodic piece and work up to a brighter song, to gently ease your child back into the world.

- *Collect an assortment.* Refresh your memory with the songs on these pages. Then add to your collection by picking up songbooks or looking through your own records. Try singing love songs to your child. Look through collections of movie scores or musicals for ideas ("Tender Shepherd" from the musical version of *Peter Pan* with Mary Martin is wonderful).

- *Don't hesitate to sing.* Your voice is your child's favorite sound. Records and tapes are no substitute for it. Cuddle your child as you sing. Let your eyes show that this is a grand experience for you as well as for him.

BRAHMS'S LULLABY

Lullaby and good night, with roses bedight,
With lilies bedecked is baby's wee bed;
Lay thee down now and rest,
May thy slumber be blest;
Lay thee down now and rest,
May thy slumber be blest.

HUSH, LITTLE BABY

Hush, little baby, don't say a word
Papa's gonna buy you a mockingbird.

If that mockingbird don't sing,
Papa's gonna buy you a diamond ring.

If that diamond ring turns brass,
Papa's gonna buy you a looking glass.

If that looking glass gets broke,
Papa's gonna buy you a billy goat.

If that billy goat won't pull,
Papa's gonna buy you a cart and bull.

If that cart and bull turn over,
Papa's gonna buy you a dog named Rover.

If that dog named Rover don't bark,
Papa's gonna buy you a horse and cart.

If that horse and cart fall down,
You'll still be the sweetest little baby in town.

ROCKABYE, BABY

Rockabye, baby, on the treetop,
When the wind blows, the cradle will rock,
When the bough breaks, the cradle will fall,
And down will come baby, cradle and all.

SLEEP, BABY, SLEEP

Sleep, baby, sleep,
Thy father guards the sheep,
Thy mother shakes the dreamland tree,
And from it fall sweet dreams for thee,
Sleep, baby, sleep.

TAPS

Day is done,
Gone the sun,
From the lake,
From the hill,
From the sky,
All is well, safely rest,
God is nigh.

STAR WISH

Star light, star bright,
First star I see tonight,
I wish I may, I wish I might,
Have the wish I wish tonight.

Why Babies Need Music

Swiss psychologist Jean Piaget spent years examining the development of children, especially how they think and learn. One of the most profoundly simple conclusions born of his years of research is that "the more a child has seen and heard, the more he wants to see and hear."

Researchers have discovered that Piaget's theory holds particular credence in the area of music. Edwin E. Gordon believes that what is absorbed unconsciously before the age of three directly affects the language development in later years. He calls this process "unconscious listening," and with his conclusions come strong admonitions to speak and sing to your child beginning at birth.

According to Gordon, a child will not develop good conscious listening abilities unless he has been exposed to speech and music before he was able to comprehend at all. Until he is a year or more, he may not be able to understand your words, but in hearing you speak, he will be developing a set of language skills that are critical to future development. By the same token, he may not understand the music you present to him, but he will be experiencing a "conditioning" that lays the foundation for later comprehension of music. Without this "unconscious listening" to a wide variety of words and sounds, his ability to grow into a conscious listener, and thus his language development, will be restricted.

As parents, we can address our children's needs by according them the same respect that we would older children; we can speak to them and sing to them as if they can hear and understand every word, every note. Sing to your child often, and especially use his name. Talk to him. Let him hear music of all varieties. The first year of his life is the most formative year in the development of receptive language (listening). Babies need music if they are ever to love music. Give your child plenty to hear, and now.

TWINKLE, TWINKLE, LITTLE STAR

Twinkle, twinkle, little star,
How I wonder what you are,
Up above the world so high,
Like a diamond in the sky;

And the traveler in the dark,
Thanks you for your friendly spark;
He would not know which way to go,
If you did not twinkle so.

When the blazing sun is set,
And the grass with dew is wet,
Then you show your little light,
Twinkle, twinkle, all the night;

And the traveler in the dark,
Thanks you for your friendly spark;
He would not know which way to go,
If you did not twinkle so.

Good-night Books

Good-night books are special books for reading aloud together. Your child will soon recite the simple words of the text with you as he grows drowsy and you do your best to stay awake.

Berger, Terry. *Ben's ABC Day.* Photos by Alice Kandell. New York: Lothrop, Lee and Shepard, 1982. A photo story of Ben's day of activities named by letters of the alphabet.

Brown, Margaret Wise. *Goodnight Moon.* Illustrated by Clement Hurd. New York: Harper and Row, 1947. This beloved classic can be read to children as young as one year. Children love to say good night to their favorite things after they hear about bunny bidding good night to the objects in his room.

————. *A Child's Good Night Book.* Illustrated by Jean Charlot. New York: Addison-Wesley, 1950. All the animals get ready for bed and, finally, children say their prayers.

Field, Eugene. *Wynken, Blynken, and Nod.* Illustrated by Barbara Cooney. New York: Hastings House, 1964. This tale of the nighttime adventures of three fishermen has delighted children and lulled them to sleep for almost a hundred years.

Hoban, Russell. *Bedtime for Frances.* Illustrated by Garth Williams. New York: Harper and Row, 1960. Frances is a friendly badger who knows as many ways to delay going to bed as any child.

Hopkins, Lee Bennett. *Go to Bed! A Book of Bedtime Poems.* New York: Alfred A. Knopf, 1979. Your child will recognize in these poems familiar themes of fear of the dark and stalling for time before going to bed.

Hutchins, Pat. *Good-Night Owl!* Boston: Macmillan, 1972. Owl's sleeping habits are out of synch with the other forest animals. Their daytime noises disturb his sleep, but at night the tables turn.

Kuskin, Karla. *Night Again.* Boston: Little Brown, 1981. These poetic illustrations of bedtime activities are particularly well suited to the younger child.

Marzollo, Jean. *Close Your Eyes.* Illustrated by Susan Jeffers. New York: Dial Press, 1978. Exquisite illustrations tell the story first of a lullabye, then of a daughter reluctantly persuaded by her father to go to bed.

Polushkin, Maria. *Mother, Mother I Want Another.* Illustrated by Diane Dawson. New York: Crown, 1978. Mother mouse thinks her baby wants another mother, but what he wants is another kiss.

Seuss, Dr. *Dr. Seuss' Sleep Book.* New York: Random House, 1962. The great storyteller tells of all the sleepwalkers and "sleep talkers" who desperately want to get to sleep.

Sharmat, Marjorie. *Goodnight Andrew, Goodnight Craig.* Illustrated by Mary Chalmers. New York: Harper and Row, 1969. Two boys delay going to sleep with typical boyish antics.

Wood, Audry. *Moonflute.* Illustrated by Don Wood. La Jolla, California: Green Tiger Press, 1980. Firen goes on a magical trip in the moonlight with a moonflute. Perfect for three- to five-year-olds.

Zolotow, Charlotte. *The Sleepy Book.* Illustrated by Vladimir Bodri. New York: Lothrop, 1958. What do pigeons, bears, fish, and moths do when they get sleepy, and where do they go? Ms. Zolotow explains and tells what children do, too.

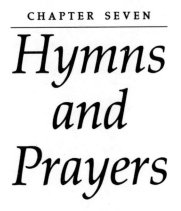

CHAPTER SEVEN

Hymns and Prayers

"Those who sing, pray twice."
—St. Augustine

INTRODUCTION

Maria Montessori writes in *The Child in the Family:* "There are clear rules to follow for physical hygiene but the rules for spiritual hygiene extend into the larger realm and are yet to be understood." In a way this book is about your child's spiritual hygiene. Not in a theological sense, but in the sense that your child has a sacred part that needs more attention than his closet or even his belly.

As much as your child needs you to be a cook or a shoe-tier or a handholder, it is the poet in you that will set you apart. And just because we are *not* poets does not mean we cannot recite or sing poetry. Your child needs your voice, and he needs you to express that there are important things in life, things that matter. This final section *is* about things that matter, prayers and hymns that have been sung and said by American children for generations.

There are magnificent treasures in this collection, songs you remember, such as "Amazing Grace" and "Swing Low, Sweet Chariot." There is the Twenty-third Psalm, which should be spoken fresh every time, and with wonder. In all, it is a tiny collection, but it is filled with jewels. I suggest you use it as a starting point and then cull music and prayers from your own church or temple or Sunday school.

I am convinced that the only way parents can share their love for God is by their own example and by sharing the great voices of their faith. Like any love, the love for God cannot be forced. But if you tell the extraordinary parables of the Bible, if you keep prayer and ritual alive in your home, and if you sing the songs of your faith with brightness and spirit, you will, like an angel, have done your part.

Here, then, with joy and reverence and faith, are a few words to start with.

THE LORD'S PRAYER

Our Father, who art in heaven,
Hallowed be Thy name.
Thy kingdom come,
Thy will be done,
On earth as it is in heaven.
Give us this day our daily bread,
And forgive us our trespasses,
As we forgive those who trespass against us.
And lead us not into temptation
But deliver us from evil.
(For Thine is the kingdom,
And the power, and the glory,
Forever.)
Amen.

AVE MARIA

Hail Mary, full of grace,
The Lord is with Thee.
Blessed art Thou among women,
And blessed is the fruit of Thy womb,
Jesus.
Holy Mary, Mother of God,
Pray for us sinners now
And at the hour of our death.
Amen.

NOW I LAY ME DOWN TO SLEEP

Now I lay me down to sleep,
I pray Thee, Lord, Thy child to keep.
Thy love go with me all the night,
And wake me with the morning light.

GOD IS GREAT

God is great,
God is good,
Let us thank Him for our food.
Amen.

GOD BE IN MY HEAD

God be in my head,
  And in my understanding;
God be in my eyes,
  And in my looking;
God be in my mouth,
  And in my speaking;
God be in my heart,
  And in my thinking;
God be at my end,
  And at my departing.

—*from* The Sarum Primer

FOR WHAT WE ARE
ABOUT TO RECEIVE

For what we are about to receive
May the Lord make us truly thankful.
Amen.

I SEE THE MOON

I see the moon,
*   And the moon sees me;*
God bless the moon,
*   And God bless me.*

THANK YOU FOR
THE WORLD SO SWEET

Thank You for the world so sweet;
Thank You for the food we eat;
Thank You for the birds that sing;
Thank you, God, for everything!

—E. Rutter Leatham

ALL THINGS BRIGHT
AND BEAUTIFUL

All things bright and beautiful,
  All creatures great and small,
All things wise and wonderful,
  The Lord God made them all.

Each little flower that opens,
  Each little bird that sings,
He made their glowing colors,
  He made their tiny wings.

The purple-headed mountain,
  The river running by,
The sunset and the morning
  That brightens up the sky,

The cold wind in the winter,
  The pleasant summer sun,
The ripe fruits in the garden,
  He made them every one.

He gave us eyes to see them,
  And lips that we might tell
How great is God Almighty,
  Who has made all things well.

—Mrs. Cecil Francis Alexander,
1848

THE TWENTY-THIRD PSALM

The Lord is my shepherd; I shall not want.
He maketh me to lie down in green pastures; He leadeth me beside still waters,
He restoreth my soul: He leadeth me in the paths of righteousness for His
name's sake.
Yea, though I walk through the valley of the shadow of death, I will fear no
evil: for Thou art with me; Thy rod and Thy staff they comfort me.
Thou preparest a table before me in the presence of mine enemies: Thou
anointest my head with oil; my cup runneth over.
Surely goodness and mercy shall follow me all the days of my life: and I will
dwell in the house of the Lord forever.

WE GATHER TOGETHER

We gather together to ask the Lord's blessing;
He hastens and chastens His will to make known;
The wicked oppressing now cease from distressing;
Sing praises to His Name, He forgets not His own.

Beside us to guide us, our God with us joining,
Ordaining, maintaining His kingdom divine;
So from the beginning the fight we were winning;
Thou, Lord, wast at our side, all glory be Thine.

We all do extol Thee, Thou Leader triumphant,
And pray that Thou still our Defender wilt be.
Let Thy congregation escape tribulation;
Thy Name be ever praised! O Lord, Make us free!
Amen.

—Translated from the Dutch by Theodore Baker

HE'S GOT THE WHOLE WORLD IN HIS HANDS

He's got the whole world in His hands,
He's got the whole wide world in His hands,
He's got the whole world in His hands,
He's got the whole world in His hands.

He's got the little bitty baby in His hands,
He's got the little bitty baby in His hands,
He's got the little bitty baby in His hands,
He's got the whole world in His hands.

He's got you and me, brother, in His hands,
He's got you and me, brother, in His hands,
He's got you and me, brother, in His hands,
He's got the whole world in His hands.

He's got you and me, sister, in His hands,
He's got you and me, sister, in His hands,
He's got you and me, sister, in His hands,
He's got the whole world in His hands.

KUM BA YA

CHORUS:
Kum ba ya, my Lord, kum ba ya.
Kum ba ya, my Lord, kum ba ya.
Kum ba ya, my Lord, kum ba ya.
Oh, Lord, kum ba ya.

Someone's crying, Lord, kum ba ya,
Someone's crying, Lord, kum ba ya,
Someone's crying, Lord, kum ba ya,
Oh, Lord, kum ba ya.

Someone's singing, Lord, kum ba ya,
Someone's singing, Lord, kum ba ya,
Someone's singing, Lord, kum ba ya,
Oh, Lord, kum ba ya.

Someone's praying, Lord, kum ba ya,
Someone's praying, Lord, kum ba ya,
Someone's praying, Lord, kum ba ya,
Oh, Lord, kum ba ya.

Someone's hoping, Lord, kum ba ya,
Someone's hoping, Lord, kum ba ya,
Someone's hoping, Lord, kum ba ya,
Oh, Lord, kum ba ya.
Repeat CHORUS

Additional verses are easily coined.

AMAZING GRACE

Amazing grace! How sweet the sound
That saved a wretch like me!
I once was lost but now am found,
Was blind, but now I see.

'Twas grace that taught my heart to fear,
And grace my fears relieved;
How precious did that grace appear,
The hour I first believed!

Through many dangers, toils, and snares,
I have already come;
'Tis grace hath brought me safe thus far,
And grace will lead me home.

The Lord hath promised good to me,
His word my hope secures;
He will my shield and portion be
As long as life endures.
—John Newton
  (1725–1807)

BATTLE HYMN OF THE REPUBLIC

Mine eyes have seen the glory
of the coming of the Lord;
He is trampling out the vintage
where the grapes of wrath are stored;
He hath loosed the fateful lightning
of His terrible swift sword;
His truth is marching on.

Glory! glory, hallelujah!
Glory! glory, hallelujah!
Glory! glory, hallelujah!
His truth is marching on.

I have seen Him in the watchfires
of a hundred circling camps;
They have builded Him an altar in
the evening dews and damps;
I can read His righteous sentence
by the dim and flaring lamps;
His truth is marching on.

Glory! glory, hallelujah!
Glory! glory, hallelujah!
Glory! glory, hallelujah!
His truth is marching on.

—Julia Ward Howe
(1819–1910)

SWING LOW, SWEET CHARIOT

Swing low, sweet chariot,
  Comin' for to carry me home,
Swing low, sweet chariot,
  Comin' for to carry me home.

I looked over Jordan and what did I see,
  Comin' for to carry me home,
A band of angels comin' after me,
  Comin' for to carry me home.

Swing low, sweet chariot,
  Comin' for to carry me home,
Swing low, sweet chariot,
  Comin' for to carry me home.

If you get up there before I do,
  Comin' for to carry me home,
Tell all my friends that I'm a-comin', too,
  Comin' for to carry me home.

Swing low, sweet chariot,
  Comin' for to carry me home,
Swing low, sweet chariot,
  Comin' for to carry me home.

Index

Index
Index of Works Included